# THE
# BIKER'S
# GUIDE TO
# BUSINESS

## WHEN BUSINESS AND LIFE MEET AT THE CROSSROADS

## DWAIN DeVILLE

**WILEY**

John Wiley & Sons, Inc.

Published by John Wiley & Sons, Inc., Hoboken, New Jersey.
Published simultaneously in Canada.

For general information on our other products and services or for technical support, please contact our Customer Care Department within the United States at (800) 762-2974, outside the United States at (317) 572-3993 or fax (317) 572-4002.

Wiley also publishes its books in a variety of electronic formats. Some content that appears in print may not be available in electronic books. For more information about Wiley products, visit our web site at www.wiley.com.

*Library of Congress Cataloging-in-Publication Data:*

DeVille, Dwain, 1955-
  The biker's guide to business : when business and life meet at the crossroads / Dwain DeVille.
      p. cm.
  Includes index.
  ISBN 978-0-470-48120-2 (cloth : acid-free paper)
  1. Success in business.   2. Leadership.   3. Communication.   I. Title.
  HF5386.D468 2009
  658.4'09–dc22

                                                              2009007399

Printed in the United States of America.

10  9  8  7  6  5  4  3  2  1

To Merrick and Bessie: You taught by example and instilled a work ethic that's served your boy well all these years. I wish you were here to see the result.

# CONTENTS

 PREFACE

## Biking and Business

Statistics show that of the 1.3 million motorcycles sold annually, over 300,000 are purchased by executive-level businessmen and businesswomen. They make up one of the largest segments of biking today: the **business biker**.

So if you're one of the millions of **business bikers**, you've picked up this book because you *get* it. You understand the rush and sense of freedom biking gives you. It's a total escape. As Leo Keily, CEO of Molson Coors, once told me, "I'm now landlocked in Colorado, so to me it's an instant sailing trip where I go to clear my head."

And while riding a motorcycle is a great way to clear the mind after a long day or week in the office, this book is not just about that. This book is not only about how I use my motorcycle to escape business, but also about how I've taken the lessons learned from a lifetime of riding and applied them to building a successful business, as well as a successful life.

To that end, this book is written for the biker and nonbiker alike who are struggling to find the right balance in business and life. For too long, entrepreneurs have accepted that their business performance and their personal lives were an either-or proposition. Like far too many entrepreneurs, I struggled to find the key to having my company work for me instead of me always working for it. Although it took a while, I created a process that allows me to perform at the highest level in business without my success coming at the expense of my personal life. I just happened to do it with the help of my bike.

The first time I straddled a motorcycle with the intent to ride, I was 16, and in a lot of ways I've never gotten off that bike. In fact, aside from family and friends, the only thing I love more than the great game of business is riding my motorcycle. Over the years motorcycling has been an integral part of my life story and continues to be a source of enlightenment and happiness. I've also come to understand that the skills and abilities it takes to be successful on a bike also come in handy when building a successful business.

To start with, both biking and business are equally thrilling and serve as vehicles to take me where I want to go, one physically and the other economically. Also, achieving excellence in each requires many skills, not the least of which are awareness, timing, and a keen ability to sift through the background noise and bullshit around you.

To be sure, a car can take me there, but what's the fun in that? In my car I'm talking on the phone, listening to the radio or a book on tape, and thinking about a million things, such as "Am I there yet?" But on my motorcycle I'm a major part of getting there. Senses totally in the moment, I'm shifting, constantly looking out for those crazy cagers (car drivers) and other road hazards. I'm literally *riding* the ride!

Nonriders immediately focus on the dangers, but there's so much more to riding and the benefits offset the risks. By hopping in the saddle and exposing my relatively unprotected body to the outside world, I literally inject myself into the environment around me as I roll along. I fully experience the sounds, take in the 180-degree view, feel the air, smell the rain right before it hits, and know that it and the bugs begin to sting at 50 miles per hour. Riding releases my senses and is the essence of truly being alive.

And the same holds true for me as an entrepreneur, because there's no greater ride than that of business. Getting out there and exposing my relatively unprotected product or service to the marketplace allows me to still feel like that 19-year-old kid just starting out; I'm ready to ride the twists and turns of the marketplace and chase the possibilities of the day.

I'll admit there are inherent risks in both biking and business. As we've all seen, if not ridden properly, each can and will cause severe damage. And if that level of risk wasn't enough, when I started out in both endeavors, my well-meaning family and friends, who feared for my bodily and financial safety, literally said to my face or behind my back that I was destined to wipe out or fail totally. To which I simply shrugged and, like any good biker or entrepreneur, went on down the road.

As a biker and entrepreneur, I know the risk and it is always with me. But riding a motorcycle scared is a fast ticket to the hospital, and for a lot of the same reasons, you damn sure can't run a company scared. Those who do know this—the champions— get that it's not about *overcoming* fear but about *understanding* and *embracing* it.

In order to truly succeed at both biking and business, I must accept many things, the first of which is reasonable and controllable risk. For me, risk goes beyond simple thrill seeking— reasonable and controllable risk is my way of life. It's my drug, my mistress, and my salvation all rolled up into one. It fits me like a $10,000 suit and I cannot fathom life without it.

Where others see risk, I see potential and innately understand that the reward at the end of the day corresponds to the amount I am willing to risk in order to achieve success. I don't simply do business—I grab it by the handlebars and ride it for all its worth!

And I'm not alone. Like bikers, entrepreneurs are today's cowboys and we are a bold lot. We're independent, adventurous, strong willed, and downright intolerant of fences—it's in our DNA. When we walk into the room, we're the alpha dogs exuding the confidence that lets everyone know we mean business. Our self-assurance comes from a burning desire to carve our own path and a belief deep down in our soul that we have a better idea and the ability to go for it.

And we know each other when we meet. There's no secret handshake, just a revealing look in our eyes that tells the other we understand. That we've both felt the highs and lows of getting where we are today and paid our dues without reservation. At some point in the beginning of our careers, we have awakened at 2:30 A.M. on a Friday in a cold sweat trying to figure out how to meet that week's payroll. And at some point, we have viewed our bank balance not as a safety net but as a down payment on a really cool new venture.

A great example of this is a biker and former client who I'll call C.J. We came together at a difficult time when his extremely competitive industry was radically shifting due to rapidly changing technology.

He joined a group of CEOs I worked with on a monthly basis and over the course of six months set about strategizing and writing a bold new business plan for his company. It was extremely innovative and showed tremendous forethought and promise. After completing the plan, he made about 30 copies and began handing them out to anyone who would read it for feedback.

One day during our meeting, a fellow CEO asked, "Aren't you afraid that other people may take your idea and implement it?" Not missing a beat, C.J. looked that person dead in the eye and said, "Maybe so, but at the end of the day they still have to beat me at it."

That's biker attitude. It's that subtle swagger that comes when you possess the supreme confidence that where your competition is good, you're better. It comes from being comfortable on the edge and knowing how to execute your plans in such a way that no one can stop you.

And that's why I believe biking makes me a better businessperson. Aside from the thrill of not having a safety net, it's my way of maintaining an edge as well as a proper perspective on business and life. More than just a metaphor for how I live, biking allows me to approach business full out and understand its edge, which is where the real jazz is.

As John Paul DeJoria, a biker and the CEO and founder of John Paul Mitchell Systems and Patrón Tequila, told me, *"The difference between successful people and unsuccessful people is that successful people do all the things unsuccessful people don't want to do."*

So saddle up alongside me and I'll show you, step by step, how I grab business and life by the handlebars!

 ACKNOWLEDGMENTS

My sincere thanks to all the mentors I've met along the way. Your lessons left an indelible impression on me, and without your touch, my ride would have been far different.

And undying gratitude to Christine for showing me *what*, Brett for showing me *how*, Chris for showing me *why*, and Shannon for helping me put it all together, stay focused, and cross those finish lines.

Had I missed any one of you on my journey, none of this would have been possible.

 CHAPTER 1

# Who Am I?

If ever there was a gym rat of business, it would be me. I absolutely love working and getting involved in any kind of selling or production. My earliest memories as a kid growing up in the 1960s were of spending my summers hanging around at and eventually working in the cotton gin my dad managed in our hometown of Opelousas, Louisiana. My mother worked (which was not so common in those days) for the largest privately owned department store in town. She managed the ladies' department while also serving as its buyer, a position that filled our evenings with the talk of business and, in particular, management. It was during these discussions about my parents' trials, tribulations, and successes that I first learned of miscommunications, backroom politics, "stupid management decisions," and employees who "didn't get it."

Right or wrong, my mother and father's insight and perspective on business framed the way in which I tend to approach and learn about it. Little did I know at the time how much those nightly lessons would fuel my hunger for business. I became extremely anxious to jump in and play the game myself. So when the time came, instead of following everyone else my age and pushing for that MBA, I decided to strap on the pads and start earning my chops in the business world.

And that's why, one month after graduating high school, I packed everything I owned onto my Honda 350 motorcycle and moved from my hometown to the big city of New Orleans. My first position was as a hand in the oil fields, and a year and a half into that job, I witnessed a scenario that rang a bell in my mind, altering my path and changing my life forever.

On one particular day, our crew was working on a job for one of the major oil companies and, honestly, doing a very poor job of it. So when their representative showed up on the job after his three-martini lunch and began berating my supervisor and everyone else within earshot, I was hit with my first of many epiphanies. As I sat there on that stack of pipe in the 95-degree heat that is New Orleans in the summer and watched this guy totally lose it, I asked myself a fundamental question: How is it that this drunken idiot in his short-sleeved shirt and tie made it into a position of authority? Hell, I can do *that*—and probably do it better—so why am I wasting my time here?

It wasn't long after witnessing this encounter that I cut my hair, bought a suit at Sears, and ventured out to carve my own path in the business world. I got myself hired by a national small loan company as a collector. I rose quickly through the ranks, became assistant manager, and then waited another six months to make manager, simply because I was not 21 years old yet and the company couldn't bond me until I was old enough.

So right after my 21st birthday, I was promoted to the position of branch manager, and I began to learn firsthand what it was like to run an office and manage a staff. It was a great time in my life; together with my staff, I began to win award after award for productivity, which only served to intensify my ambition and feed my hubris. In fact, I began to grow an ego the size of the Crescent City and quickly became a handful to manage myself. But under the subtle guidance of my district supervisor and mentor, I also began to learn. As with anything, some lessons came easily and naturally, but others were tough.

Of all the important lessons he taught me, probably the greatest lesson of all was that *knowledge isn't power until you apply it.* The key to ultimate success is to apply what you've learned effectively. I quickly realized that I needed to check my oversized ego at the door in order to apply what I had learned through others.

This important lesson stayed with me as through the years I worked with company after company, in management position after management position. (I was, and continue to be, a restless wanderer.) I learned by doing, reading, listening, and watching—all the while, stretching my limits. Combined with my natural biker instincts, this constant need to grow allowed me to absorb all that was around me, while continuing to ask the tough questions that cut through the bullshit and see the real game.

My road eventually led to a career in banking where I really earned my business chops by helping to turn around distressed banks and work through mergers for the better part of 15 years. John, my first boss in that world, was a no-nonsense bank president who wasn't a biker but should have been. He was *the* major turnaround guy in a company of turnaround guys. Tough as nails, focused, and determined, John personally taught me how to take an organization on the verge of collapse and turn it into a winner. This was no easy feat; we had to transform failing banks while retaining the same group of bankers that ran them into the ditch in the first place. After all, banking is a very conservative industry, and no banker in his or her right mind is going to leave a position in a sound institution to join one on the verge of collapse.

I began my apprenticeship in the mid-1980s under John's supervision. I was recruited to help restore a small bank in Houma, Louisiana, where the principal industry is oil, which was in the tank, so to speak, hitting an all-time low price of $11 a barrel. (The good old days, eh?) Having assumed control one year prior to my joining the institution, the bank was a distant third in a three-bank race and was losing ground quickly.

What made the challenge even more interesting was the state of the economy; there was little to no economic growth from which to turn a bank around. So we became predators, and through John's guidance and leadership, we became the only bank to show solid growth by literally taking business away from the other two.

I watched as John spent much of his time doggedly communicating his vision to everyone in the organization. He set a clear course and made sure that all the employees in the organization knew their roles and, perhaps more importantly, understood how their efforts were contributing to the overall cause. John's communication style was relentlessly straightforward and at times forcefully so. He let nothing slide; even though you might not have always liked his delivery, you *always* understood the message. That was a critical lesson I took with me going forward: Everything in business is dependent on clear and consistent communication.

And it was with John in mind that I coined my favorite and most often-used saying: *"Communication ain't always pretty, but it's always communication."*

After that two-year master's level course in turnaround management, I eventually left Louisiana for merger-frenzied Florida. It seemed that every bank was either buying or being bought by another. Hell, in the eight years I remained in the business, the bank name on my business card changed five times without my ever really changing employers.

That job was a blast, though, and I remained in constant turnaround mode—getting office after office out of trouble and having the time of my life. Utilizing all the tricks that John had taught me, I focused on identifying and recruiting great talent, placing these people in the right spots, and then relentlessly communicating our mission and their role in it. Unfortunately, all good things must come to an end, and as luck would have it, at the age of 38, the frenzy died down and my banking career fizzled—simply because I began to get very bored.

That was also around the time when my midlife "passage" kicked in and I began to wonder what else was out there for me beyond banking. Midlife is generally known as the time when you stop the presses, take stock of who you are and what you do, and reconfigure where it is you want to go. It's when you tend to ask for a do-over or, in my case, an entirely new direction.

So I shunned conventional wisdom, left the false security of corporate America, and went off to explore a new game that eventually led me to build my consulting business.

Now, I wouldn't necessarily recommend that you leave a successful 15-year career to go off and begin your own company while hitting that midlife stage but it *can* be one hell of a ride. I also have a sneaking suspicion that I'm not the only person who's done so. Along the way I won a few, lost a few, and some got rained out. I went through the requisite divorce, experienced a number of spiritual awakenings and epiphanies, and learned several hard-ass lessons that lent true credence to the old saying *"that which does not kill me will make me stronger."* And each trial, whatever its end result, turned out to be a treasure trove of lessons that has given me the balls to not only go out on my own but survive and thrive in the biggest, baddest game there is.

My current career started 15 years ago when I was recruited out of banking to join a small firm that ran CEO peer group roundtables, the type where six to eight entrepreneurs from different industries come together one day a month in order to discuss an issue that they're facing and have everyone help resolve it. Early on, these very real issues seemed larger than life and left me feeling a bit intimidated. After all, it was one thing to read about these topics in a book or magazine interview, but I was actually there in the room, contributing to major decisions. It was a total rush for a business junkie like me, and more than once I had to remind myself that they were actually *paying* me to be in the room and not vice versa! It quickly became apparent, however, that the issues weren't much different from those that I'd faced during my career in banking or heard discussed at my parent's kitchen table. So once I got past my awe over what this group of CEOs had built, I found them to be regular folks who are just wired a bit differently than the rest of us.

It also didn't take long for me to recognize that I needed to create my own niche and not simply join another pack. And so, seven months into that gig, I left to go my own way and launched my very own firm. Today I serve as Navigator to a select group of successful companies while growing my own organization.

Working with these entrepreneurs intimately on a day-to-day basis gives me the opportunity to see and experience first-hand how decisions are made and how issues are dealt with—and to witness the many ways in which these professionals handle the daily fear associated with being the leader of a company. Every day I have the privilege of riding with the big dogs, and I love every minute of it. I feed off their sheer drive and determination to succeed at this level, while also sharing their fear of failure, a fear fueled by an overriding sense of responsibility to the company and their employees. Therefore, the main thing that brings us together is their want and need to find and maintain the right focus.

I've carved out a reputation as the "anti-consultant" because of the way I approach my Navigation Process. I tend to help established winners achieve their definition of success by getting them to focus more on *living* than on business, because, as I've previously stated, at the highest level, excellence in business and life show up as two sides of the same coin. *Both* must embody your true passions and support each other, as greatness only comes when you embrace the fact that your business is a true extension of who you are, while making apologies to no one for it. Your business *is* the very essence of why you do what you do.

So on the pages that follow, I'll share my story, along with a few others that will help you get to where it is you want to go safely and on time. As Bob Parsons, CEO and founder of GoDaddy.com so aptly put it, *"We're not here for a long time; we're here for a good time."*

 CHAPTER 2

# Why Am I Writing This Book?

There's an old biking adage that says there are two types of riders in this world: those who have laid it down (wiped out) and those who will. The possibility of wiping out is a fact of life and something we, as successful entrepreneurs and bikers, readily accept. I wish I had a dollar for each time someone, upon hearing that I'm a biker, tells me of the wipeout that caused him or her to never get back on the bike. The former biker always looks at me with eyes that plead for understanding that, in my case, never comes because I *don't* understand that approach. I merely chuckle, shake my head, and walk away.

My somewhat cold response doesn't come from denial of my own vulnerability or from disinterest in others' troubles, but from a difference in attitude. Although we bikers never think that a similar wipeout or misfortune will happen to us, when it does (notice I didn't say *if* ), our mettle as riders is truly tested and we come face to face with the ultimate decision: Do I get back on the bike or not? My experience as both a long-term biker and a successful entrepreneur has shown that the way in which you face that moment of truth affects not only your ability to ride, but your ability to conduct your business and life. For me, how you handle this decision speaks to your passion and whether or not you're "all in," as my poker-playing friends would say.

I say this from experience, having had my own share of severe wipeouts. In each case, I faced that moment where I questioned whether or not to get back up and onto the bike. And each time, I elected to do so, believing that wipeouts are part of life's tuition and we waste an all-important lesson if we refuse to learn from these misadventures as we continue along on our journey.

On the pages that follow are the lessons I learned when it was time for me to get back on the bike and continue to build the type of business and life I dreamed of when I was starting out. To be sure, there are some who simply don't belong on the ride and this book isn't for them. Instead, this book is for those of us who understand that success is more choice than chance, and who want to know and understand not only why we laid it down but how to get back up—and excel when doing so.

Walk into any bookstore and you'll find dozens of books on how to run your company more successfully; across the store are just as many on how to live your life more fully. (I know; I've read most of them.) What makes this book different is my fundamental belief that at the highest level there's little to no separation between our lives and the businesses we've built, that for an entrepreneur to be successful, both components must be dealt with together. They are two sides of the same coin, and it's time we stop apologizing for it.

For entrepreneurs, business and life come together to form one long road trip with many exits along the way. Each exit has its own siren song and glittering road signs filled with promises of fulfillment and excitement. *The Biker's Guide to Business* will help you navigate this road; not only will you figure out which direction to take, but you'll discover which exits will allow you to enjoy yourself while achieving success.

Success no longer means a total trade-off between your personal and professional lives; your relationships and interests don't have to suffer in order for your business to grow. Nor do you have to wait for the inevitable wipeout to learn the lessons that will allow you to make your visions of success a reality. You *can* have it both ways, but only if you understand a few fundamental techniques that are easily mastered and implemented.

Just as the lessons and methods taught at riding school can ensure a lifetime of safe biking habits, the tools and insights that fill these pages can help you excel, as they have helped me and the hundreds of successful entrepreneurs with whom I've worked. The motorcycle as metaphor is not simply a clichéd reference to risk and bravado; it's a vehicle that teaches straightforward techniques that will keep you upright and turn your ride into one where you achieve success in *both* business and life.

*The Biker's Guide to Business* also serves as an alternative to the hundreds of business books out there based solely on theory and observation. As a voracious reader of these kinds of books, I'm too often subjected to the opinions of writers who have passively observed others rather than actually *accomplishing* something themselves. Though well-meaning, their hindsight and armchair quarterbacking are gained from the sidelines. While there's some value in these recitals, I, along with many others, yearn for the true stories of real business leaders. I want to feel their pain, taste their fear, and understand with clarity how they overcame their obstacles.

Many authors have made their marks by simply regurgitating on paper what they've seen from afar, and I'm damned tired of it. The entrepreneurs with whom I work and hang out want to hear from someone whose ass is on the line day after day, facing issues that fly by at the speed of life. We want to hear from business leaders who have laid it down in a big way, and to see how they reacted. *So if you're looking for a run-of-the-mill business book based on theory and observation, this ain't it.*

Yes, there are also books written by successful former entrepreneurs that are extremely valuable. The principal issue I have with these romantic recollections from those who have made it is not with the validity of their stories; on the contrary, there's true value in their words. However, the passage of time often causes them to forget or to gloss over many of the little things that are crucial to helping someone else overcome similar problems and find success in today's fast-paced business world. Rarely do we find a book with stories and lessons from the front lines of the business world. Accordingly, we are forced to spend valuable time digesting and testing theories or recollections that have little meaning in the real world. And the reason we're at the mercy of these casual business observers is that most entrepreneurs are too damned busy *being* entrepreneurs to take the time to write about it.

When the rubber meets the road, we want and need real in-the-saddle experience that can be used *now*. We desperately require lessons from people and companies just like us as we move forward. With all due respect to Jack Welch (for I am a true fan) and the thousands of other writers who have penned their stories, what works in a behemoth like GE doesn't necessarily transfer to a company of 10, 20, or 100 people. *The Biker's Guide to Business* is specifically for entrepreneurs, and my overarching goal is to let you know that you're not alone in your day-to-day struggles. There are tons of others out there just like you who have not only survived but are *still* in the saddle riding that dream for all its worth.

I consider myself to be a typical entrepreneur; I started my business 15 years ago, survived the early stages, fought through the middle years, and am now looking to maintain that ever-elusive state of high performance in order to profit from all of the fear, heartache, and sweat it took to get here. On the pages that follow are the lessons gleaned over these 15 years, lessons that come from my own experience as well as those of the companies I work with every day. Some are raw, straightforward, and intensely personal, but in the end, each and every one proves that business is business, and every situation shares certain similarities.

But, you may ask, if I'm still fully engaged in this great ride of business and life, how can I take the time to write about it? As you might guess, both my consulting business and the writing of this book are full-time jobs. But what makes this book doable at this time is the extensive catalog of experiences I have and the stage of business and life in which I find myself. I need no further research, for I've either already lived it or am in the middle of it. I need to conduct few interviews, because for years I've worked alongside the people whose stories fill these pages.

I'm also writing this book to honor all of my clients, mentors, and business associates who have insisted that I share the trials and successes we've experienced and shared over the course of my career. They told me that if they'd had the benefit early on in their careers of one-tenth of the insight I am now able to share, they'd have reached their goals faster and achieved more over the course of their professional lives.

Therefore, it's my sincere hope that the stories and methods that follow will help you arrive where you want to go safely and successfully, because life is a fast-moving highway that should be ridden with gusto!

 CHAPTER 3

# Roadside Distractions

I've been riding a motorcycle for over three decades, and the fundamental skill that keeps me safe and upright is my ability to avoid roadside distractions. These can be hazardous to your health, and experienced riders know to keep their eyes in constant motion and their head on a "swivel" in order to see potential problems; once the problems are recognized, they also know *not to fixate on them*. This is because when you're on a bike, where you look is where the bike is going to go—so if you focus on something like a pothole or telephone pole, you'll probably hit it.

This seemingly simple skill is one of the hardest things for a new rider to master, as it differs greatly from the skills needed to drive a car. However, even the most skittish riders will eventually grasp it after spending enough time in the saddle. This ability also correlates to the speed with which you can safely roll; you tend to ride more slowly early on, because your reactions aren't quite as quick as they will be later on. The more miles you spend in the saddle, the more you understand your abilities, and you can begin to safely increase your speed as your instincts improve. That said, whatever your experience level, taking your eyes off the road will, at the very least, slow you down, and doing it at the wrong time can also begin a devastating chain of events from which you may not recover. So knowing what to focus on and at what speed is absolutely necessary to enjoying a safe journey.

In business, there are also roadside distractions that, depending on your level of experience, will either slow you down or run you off course. I speak from hard experience, and will discuss some of these distractions later in this book. However, right now I want to focus on overcoming a certain mind-set that is adopted by most entrepreneurs who are just starting out in business: the "do what it takes" attitude, which compels them to focus on distractions.

In the early days of establishing a company, your need for money and eagerness to please prompt you to take on everyone looking for your service. In order to keep the doors open, you accept any task, from anyone, at any time—and find it difficult to move forward while running from side to side (and even backwards) because of what you've agreed to do. It's *imperative* that you move past this stage as quickly as possible. Your ability to overcome this distraction determines whether you'll reach your full potential or instead remain in constant start-up mode, always on the brink of wiping out.

When I started my own business, I needed to figure out not just what I was good at, but also what I was passionate about—and then master that and just stick to it. Though I certainly possessed the acumen to write a marketing plan or full-blown business plan, it wasn't my passion. While it didn't take me long to understand that my business niche was as a Navigator of companies, the real difficulty came in figuring out how to take the bold step of refusing any project that didn't fit my passion.

I began by creating a vision statement against which all subsequent projects were measured. In order for that to work, this vision statement needed to clearly and succinctly announce to everyone exactly who I was and what I planned on accomplishing. It also had to be broad enough to stand the test of time and to allow for flexibility in the individual missions needed to carry out this vision.

I created the following statement way back then, and it has not changed by a single word in the years since.

*We are dedicated to providing an environment where leaders of growing companies can continually achieve greater profitability and breakthrough performance through shared knowledge, on-time information, and enhanced leadership.*

This simple yet powerful statement keeps me centered and grounded in my daily business life. Over time, I've found that I always struggle mightily with any project that deviates from it, while I profit greatly by staying true to it. That said, implementing it has been one of the greatest challenges in my business career.

Establishing your true place in the mind of the market takes time, staying power, and tons of intestinal fortitude. Whereas I had previously marketed multiple services to multiple pockets of customers, after I created my vision statement, I focused on only one segment of the market: CEOs of smaller entrepreneurial companies. It took the better part of a year to get that message out to a large enough portion of the market to ensure my business's survival. The good thing was that I was still "young" in business and going through the mental transition of becoming an entrepreneur after leaving the corporate world. Staying power was tough to maintain, but the fact that "I didn't know what I didn't know" helped somewhat. I drove forward with an unshakable belief that I could build something special if I could cross that finish line.

What helped me get through that phase was slowing down, taking time to reflect on what I was doing, and figuring out ways to do it better. As you go through this book, you'll find that a recurring theme is my need to get away from it all from time to time—either on the water or on the back of a bike—simply to ponder life. That's always been my style; what works best for me is to go off to a place where I can simply be alone with myself. What works for you may be different, but the principle remains the same: You must find time to get away on a regular basis and clear your mind in order to remain open to information.

At that particular time, I had a friend whose home was on the market, and for my getaway I was able to use her boathouse, which stood empty for more than four wonderful months. I spent the evening there almost every Friday, admiring the sunset and pondering the week that had passed and the one to come. To help my thought processes along, I employed a Walkman, a laptop, cigars, and a thermos of martinis.

I would settle in by pouring a martini, firing up a cigar, putting my headphones on, and opening up a file on my laptop entitled Ramblings on a Friday Night. As the sun slowly set, I would mindlessly transfer everything in my head into the file. I didn't worry about rhyme or reason, nor did I care about proper composition. This was a pure and simple brain dump designed to clear the clutter in my head and store these thoughts where I could easily find them later.

I still have that file to this day, and I can identify with certainty when the martinis kicked in. My statements got bolder and more self-assured, and my cocky side came out as I wrote down one wacky idea after another, some of which, with a tweak here or there, actually worked. But after the typing frenzy subsided and the martinis thoroughly took hold, I let my emotions flow freely. If I'd had a particularly good week, I'd literally howl at the moon or dance to the music with abandon. Conversely, if it had been a particularly scary week or total downer, I didn't hesitate to cry.

I've always believed that emotions are important pressure points and that it's essential that we embrace them in order to remain balanced. After all, you cannot fully appreciate the highs to which joy will take you in this world until you've experienced and accepted the depths of sadness.

On one particularly bad Friday night, I found myself at the edge of surrender. Understand that the last thing any self-respecting self-employed consultant wants to do is take a job as someone else's employee—something I was perilously close to doing. In the world of entrepreneurship, this has always been the ultimate mark of failure, kind of like turning 40 and having to move back in with your parents because you can't make it on your own.

My finances—or, to be more accurate, my lack thereof—had brought me to that edge. I had finished the week with around $28 in my checking account and wondered aloud if I was going to make it. It wasn't the being broke part that worried me; I'd been there before and it didn't frighten me. The question wasn't how to make money. Hell, I knew that. The real question was whether or not I could make money doing what I loved and was most passionate about. And could I do it in time to save my ass?

So, late in the evening, emboldened by the martinis and with tears in my eyes, I walked to the edge of the dock, looked to the sky, and screamed to the business gods at the top of my lungs, *"What is it going to take? I've cashed in all the stocks, run through the cash, and all that's left is the f'ing house! I'm willing to sell that, too, if you need it, because I'm not quitting. So quit screwing around and start giving back. It's time!"*

Aside from feeling really good—and possibly certifying me as nuts in public—that outburst defined for me the Law of Risk versus Reward. Simply put, this rule states that the level of success one enjoys as an entrepreneur and in life is commensurate with one's willingness to lay it on the line when necessary. It's where you stare down the business gods and let them know, in no uncertain terms, that you may be down but you're not quitting.

For me, this was a significant test of passion and focus, because I'm certain that flinching at any time would have subjected me to a lifetime of mediocrity and unfulfilled dreams.

My feedback from the business gods thankfully came quickly. The next day, I opened my post office box to find a check from a client for $2,500 and have not looked back since. Indeed, it continued to be a very hard climb, and for the better part of a year, I often paid the final bill of the month on the last day of that month. But even this gave me a strange sense of humor, and I'd wake up on the first of every month humming the old Donovan tune, "First there is a mountain, then there is no mountain, then there is." I was out of debt one day and owing thousands the next, but I was keeping my head above water and making it happen.

Unfortunately, that little test from the business gods isn't a one-time thing. The higher you climb, the more tests you encounter, since they wait for you at each plateau. Once you identify and overcome those initial roadside distractions, your pace increases. Opportunities begin to come at you faster and you can filter them better—that is, until the terrain changes. The development of your business ability is much like the evolution of your biking skills—as both improve, they allow you to ride more interesting and difficult terrain.

In your business, you begin to see connection points and natural extensions of what your company does—each one a siren song of distraction and each one holding the promise of greater revenue and profitability. However, I've come to learn that *the key to success isn't recognizing opportunity, but instead recognizing the opportunities you should not chase.*

And, as you'll see throughout this book, knowing which opportunities to bypass is easier said than done.

 CHAPTER 4

# The In-Between

Each time I ride my motorcycle, I learn valuable lessons that, when translated into my business life, make me a better and happier person. That's because jumping on two wheels and exposing my relatively unprotected body to the dangers of the outside world forces me to focus on the journey or, as I like to call it, the *in-between*.

For bikers, it's *always* about the journey rather than the destination. Because of our vulnerability, our senses are always totally in the moment; they force us to notice subtle nuances and recognize changes even though we've ridden a road a thousand times. We love and live for the in-between because it's sexy, never routine, and gives us that signature swagger. And that swagger is not just bravado. It's grounded in the knowledge and the skill that it takes to wake up, plant a flag on the map, figure out the best route, and ride.

In business, however, the in-between is viewed as anything but sexy and causes the opposite of swagger. The in-between isn't exciting; it's sweaty. It's not about dreaming; it's about doing. It is about the routine, the mundane, and the everyday. It's why most entrepreneurs now run their businesses like they're driving a car—doing it while they're on the phone, listening to the radio or a book on tape, and thinking about a million things—the least of which is the road you're traveling on, because you drive it each and every day. After a while, the next road looks just like the last one with the same street lights, shops, and restaurants along the way. And because you're in an environmentally controlled cage, you have no idea which way the wind is blowing and no true sense of what's in the air, causing you to miss the subtle changes along the way.

To put it into a business context, you walk into your office every day and, for the most part, go about your duties in the same way. This new customer is the same as the last, with similar wants and needs. The problems you face are also similar, and the sheer routine of it all makes the business for which you once felt such intense passion boring and monotonous. You've encased yourself and your company in an environmentally controlled bubble of sameness.

Another factor that makes the in-between no longer as sexy is the fact that it flies in the face of the instant-gratification world in which we now live. In other words, I'm here, but I want to be there. The in-between? Fuggedaboutit because I want to get there *now*!

We come to believe that strategy wins out, and the in-between is simply where all the messy details and potholes lie on the road to success. We think that dwelling on these mundane minutiae will keep us up at night instead of letting us *dream*. After all, the latest New Age books I read don't mention anything about the in-between. They all tell me that the secret to success is to simply meditate on my goals long enough and keep my eyes on the prize—and it will simply *come* to me.

If you think I'm off base, then test it. Ask any business leaders and they can easily tell you where they are today and most can also paint a pretty picture of where they want to be in the future, somewhere over that beautiful, bright horizon. You'll have found winners, though, if they can *also* describe the in-between. These leaders know the importance of returning that one phone call, sending that one e-mail, or scheduling that one meeting. They routinely take care of all the little things that could be pushed off until tomorrow, because they understand the value of staying in touch with the supposed small stuff.

The great Peter Drucker once wrote that "Size does not equal significance," confirming that worrying about the little things you need to do on a daily basis is crucial to your navigating the in-between. Not focusing on these small, seemingly insignificant tasks today is the cause of missed deadlines or an order falling through the cracks tomorrow. To be sure, it is extremely difficult to quantify the impact of waiting until tomorrow to send that e-mail or return that phone call. But I ask that you consider the importance of these details when you miss your next goal by one day, or when you find yourself buried as deadline after deadline crashes down around you.

The real danger to your organization's health in embracing the strategic mind-set comes when you and your employees focus more on the prize than on the path, causing everyone to value the big "Aha!" over the routine. Not completing the tasks that comprise the routine will eventually slow down the best-run organizations and devastate the not-so-well-run organizations. This is why I refer to it as *The Tragedy of Strategy.*

 CHAPTER 5

# The Tragedy
# of Strategy

Don't get me wrong; I believe that strategy is important, I really do. But I refuse to dwell on it. Instead, I'll take for granted that your strategy is sound, because entrepreneurs are naturally good at it. Hell, the dot-com boom of the late 1990s proved that. Back then, killer strategies were everywhere; many legendary strategies were written on a scratch pad or the back of a napkin over a few drinks, and then received tons of investment dollars. But few actually made it, because they were all form with no substance. They were great ideas with no real plan for what it would take to make these ideas actionable.

Listen to the experts, and it's all about strategy. That's because strategy is big and sexy; strategy lets you dream, be bold, and go for it! Today, you are told to think globally, restructure your business model, study the competition, and forecast where the marketplace is heading. So you hire big-time consultants, bring together the best and brightest from your organization, hole up in meeting rooms for days, rework the mission statement, and produce this big honking binder called a *plan*. You then hold an all-hands meeting to announce it and get everyone on the same page. Yelling "Charge!" you hand a copy to everyone and still miss the mark. Why?

Like students who graduate college with initials after their names and believe that they've totally made it only to find that the game's just begun, you too are going through an exhausting and often futile exercise. You spend so much time preparing to prepare, talking about your strategy, and covering every conceivable angle that it leaves everyone wrung out from the experience. And as for the actual *plan* that comes out of this process? Well, that's for the employees to execute; it was only your job to think it up. All they have to do is read the brilliance on all of these pages and (somehow) make it happen. Turn one page at a time and all will work out.

Then six months into the year, you wake up and smell the exhaust fumes as your competitor passes you by. Behind in your goals and woefully off track, you again turn to the experts who say that what you need now is a new, *revised* plan. Aside from the fact that it's often a boondoggle for the client company and a great way for consultants to get into the company coffers (that is, it's profitable), strategy feeds our intellectual side. It's so much more rewarding and fun to talk about it and pontificate than it is to actually *do* anything. It gives us conversation over coffee and allows us to display brilliance at the meeting table. After all, from time to time we're all legends in our own mind; strategy gives us the sense that we're on top of things, while the company is slowly drifting off course.

But the fact is that business simply doesn't work that way. If it did, then all of those plans written on napkins would have worked out beautifully and there would be, as my dad used to say, "more billionaires on *Forbes*'s vaunted list than you could shake a stick at."

A prime example of the downfall of this strategic mind-set took place early in my career. I began working for a client who was desperately looking for a way to gain market share against her main competitor, the 10,000-pound gorilla in her market. At the time, Lisa's company revenues were steady at the $7 million mark, while her competitor, Julie, sat at $60 million.

When I walked into Lisa's office, she was in the process of going to every company her competitor had under contract and severely undercutting its prices, while offering the same services. This, she soon found out, was a loser's game, because Julie, the competitor simply went back in, matched her price, and maintained market share. This left my client feeling defeated and literally wanting to sell her company at any price.

It was then I asked Lisa, "Why are you fighting this losing battle? Is there a space in the market that the gorilla is completely ignoring?" It turned out that there were quite a few options, so for the next several years, my client changed her tactics and introduced new product after new product into the market. In doing so, she gained considerable market share and momentum, resulting in $12 million of growth in a mere 14-month period.

Now, the twist here is that the tragedy in this strategy didn't lie in my client's approach, but rather in that of her competitor, the $60 million industry leader. It seems that Julie, the CEO of the competing company, was quite pleased with her own strategic approach to beating her smaller competitor. And if the standard of success was keeping her clients, she was successful. But Julie failed to consider one key question: At what cost? With her eyes fixed only on the prize, Julie failed to look at the ramifications of cutting her prices so deeply year after year, and over time, the company began to bleed financially. You see, along with introducing new products, Lisa continued to lowball the competitor, knowing full well that she'd not get the business. This simple tactic trumped Julie's ongoing strategy and allowed Lisa to enter the market through a side door.

By the time Julie recognized the problem, it was too late, and the company literally closed its doors and ceased to exist within three years of Lisa's initial attack. Over the next several years,

Lisa methodically grew her company into a $50 million market leader before merging into a publicly traded company—allowing her to retire to a villa on the water.

This is not an isolated example. While the competitor's failure does seem, on the surface, to be simply a result of flawed strategy, on some levels, the competitor's strategy was sound. The problem was that she thought the game ended with merely keeping her clients. She failed to sense the opportunity in the wind and create new products to drive through her captive market.

That's precisely why I focus so intently on the in-between. This is the place that displays all of the warning signs that, if ignored, will always lead to your company's demise. In biking, we are taught something called the *crash ladder*. This is a maxim that lists the factors which, if controlled while riding, will prevent you from ever going down. Failure to pay attention to even one or two on your ride causes your risk of crashing to rise considerably. On a bike, these factors are made up of little things, such as looking through a curve and not outrunning your headlights at night. In business, similarly modest details can make a difference, such as understanding your market and paying attention to margins. But unlike in biking, where the factors are universal, in business the factors are often unique to the company and its industry.

So how do you avoid this *Tragedy of Strategy* and achieve more of what you want? Well, to paraphrase politics of a few years ago, *"It's the tactics, stupid!"* It boils down to identifying the small stuff. And contrary to a popular slogan of a few years ago, in business, *we do have to sweat the small stuff!*

Yes, for the most part, we all have a grip on the little things, or else we wouldn't be where we are today. But the reality is that the number of issues swirling around daily within your company makes it nearly impossible for you and your organization to maintain that grip on growth. To better preserve the proper focus and control, you simply need to identify and map out the key items, both large and small, that are crucial to successfully navigating your chosen route. Applying a process to them and consistently watching the results will help you to stay on top of those critical day-to-day tasks.

In other words, there should be no big "Aha!s" along your route. Talk to any good bikers and they will tell you how important it is for there to be few, if any, big "Aha!s" along the way. That's because a surprise like this usually spells trouble and signals the fact that we didn't take the time to understand and account for all known factors along our ride. And that can be hazardous to our health.

This is why we break down our ride into one leg of the trip at a time and assume an attitude of wary confidence that serves to guide our decisions. That way, we're ready when the sun goes behind the clouds and forces us to ride through a major detour or an afternoon downpour. Slogging through it ain't fun and we'd love to go faster, but at least we're still safely going for it.

The main points to remember are that no ride happens without performance, and that success always lies in the tactics because every road is riddled with obstacles that will toss you in a ditch if not navigated properly. And in business, misunderstanding and failing to master the necessary tactics to get from here to there won't just throw you into the proverbial ditch. It is, in fact, where even the *best* strategies go to *die*.

 CHAPTER 6

# What is Navigation?

*Business moves at the speed of life.*

Throughout this book I talk about the Navigation Process and refer to myself as a Navigator. This is because, over the years, I've come to recognize that running my company, or any company, is akin to taking a long road trip on a bike. Any experienced biker will tell you that the key to arriving at your destination successfully and on time is skillful handling of the in-between that separates here from there.

For a decade and a half, I have successfully used my Navigation Process to grow not only my own company, but those of my clients. Now, this isn't Business 101, as the entrepreneurs I work with are already good at what they do. However, they all have different needs. Some still want to dominate their markets, but without working so hard; others have reached that inevitable crossroads where business intersects life, and they need to figure out the direction to take.

On average, my clients have been in business for over 30 years, lead successful companies, and are proven winners. However, decades of being in the saddle has left them suffering from a form of trail fatigue and looking for options. They've reached an intersection and find it difficult to move forward; this roadblock tends to confuse them because at this stage of their careers, they are used to achieving what they put their minds to.

I say *confuse* because these people are all really good at what they do and are not familiar with this type of roadblock. They come in to work every day and give the same effort as before (in many cases, too much), but just can't gain the traction needed to get there. They say, "We're working harder than ever, but the results just aren't coming."

They are so close to and intertwined within the business that figuring out which habits are causing this problem is nearly impossible without a different set of eyes. It's like a biker riding the same ride day after day and wondering why the view isn't changing—which is why they call me.

Our initial conversation usually begins with the client saying, "I'd like for you to help me figure out why the hell we're not where we need to be and what I need to do about it." To a degree, all conversations differ, but clients generally reveal one or more of the following symptoms that have led me to their door:

- "I'm tired."
- "I'm overwhelmed."
- "I'm constantly fighting more and larger fires."
- "I'm rarely if ever happy anymore."
- "I yearn for the good old days."
- "My team cannot keep pace with the company's rate of growth." (Or more important, that of the marketplace.)
- "We're always scrambling to meet deadlines at the last minute."
- "We're missing too many deadlines."
- "Why am I always the ultimate answer man (or woman)?"

Or my all time favorite:

- *"I'm tired and pissed off because I hired all these people to help pull the damn wagon and when I turned around they were all sitting in it!"*

Any of these sound familiar? If so, it's because getting to where you are now required years of hard work as well as many trials and trade-offs. You and your organization have established habits and norms that no longer serve the mission and are now gumming up the works. The people who work for you are now part of an extended family and over time this causes the business to take on a life of its own.

Your employees and your company became central to all that you do because they were the means to your success in life. But the years took their toll and you slowly lost sight of where it is you originally wanted to go, or due to circumstances along the way, you changed your destination altogether. The markets shifted and the trends changed along with the business—and eventually changed you.

And through it all, you've been a good steward, making mostly right decisions and putting the company first. You made personal concessions along the way, though it was no big deal. This is the game you bought into, and that's what you'd been taught was the price of admission.

Until you wake up one morning and wonder if this is all there is to life. You begin to feel stuck and in a rut. What happened to life being all about you? When did you begin to lose sight of your goals and dreams? When did you become an employee?

You want to get back in control of your life and have the business begin working for you like it was supposed to from the start. But the question is how.

That's where I come in. In the role of Navigator, I serve as strategist, tactician, mentor, teacher, coach, and above all, trusted advisor. I help my clients to stay focused on what is best for them and their company by providing an attentive ear, an open mind, and the balls to disagree when I think they are off base.

This role is vitally important because entrepreneurs at every level crave true candor and rarely get it. That's because the old adage that "it's lonely at the top" is true. Openly sharing everything on your mind to either your staff or family will only serve to confuse and scare the hell out of everyone. So that leaves you with few people to turn to for insight and straightforward feedback.

But feedback alone won't get you there. You need a new perspective on your business and how it fits into your life. Bottom line, your company is nothing more than the economic engine that will hopefully take you where it is you want to go. Metaphorically speaking, it's what you hop onto daily and ride on your long road trip to success.

And once you've come to view your company as such, you need to apply a process to it that ensures your direction is true and helps you to achieve the level of performance necessary to get to your destination on time. It comes down to doing a better job at navigating your journey.

As entrepreneurs, the ride we're most attracted to is the road less traveled, because it's much more interesting, has the best view, and challenges us. And it's the need to carve our own path that makes the ride more difficult, as we can't simply rely on an off-the-shelf GPS. Yes, through the experience of others we can begin to create our own map, but that's usually on the fly and thereby incomplete, missing many crucial route details.

Then there is simply the road that is sometimes clear, but more often than not holds many challenges that pop up in the form of twists, turns, and roadblocks. These distractions cause us to wake up one morning wondering where the hell we are and why it is we wanted to go *there* in the first place. Oh, and by the way, why aren't we *there* yet?

We begin to question our direction and ability to successfully ride *there*, which causes us to begin looking for answers everywhere. Along the way, we read books, hire consultants, and reach out to mentors and advisors, accumulating reams of information. But in the end, all of the information gathered over the course of our life and career must be digested and analyzed in order to get there. And this is where Navigation comes in.

My Navigation Process is designed specifically for these "What now?" moments. What makes it unique is its single-minded focus on having your business work toward your life goals. It clearly identifies the work to be done, along with the necessary plans, activities, conversations, and skills.

For the past 15 years, this simple yet powerful approach to execution has delivered successful results within a diverse cross section of entrepreneurial companies. Based on proven fundamentals, the process relies on focus and consistency rather than speed, because excellence comes when performance is sustained over time.

Each section of the process is designed to easily adapt to the day-to-day workings of your organization, not disrupt it. It helps you to harness that all-important "do what it takes" attitude and turns your organization into a consistent top performer.

In the chapters that follow, I will show you how to achieve your goals faster by running your company as if you were biking on a long road. Much like the biker who's riding cross-country, you need to do more than just point to a spot on the map and ride. Before lifting the kickstand on your business, it's important to figure out and focus on six things.

## 1. The Ultimate Destination

Every successful trip begins with the destination in mind, and in Chapter 7 I introduce you to *The Question*, which will help you to determine where it is you want to go in life. You are probably wondering why I'm discussing life first—isn't this a business book?

That's because it is my firm belief that life and business are two sides of the same coin, and you cannot achieve meaningful success in either unless both are taken into account at the very beginning of the planning stage.

To do this, you must place your life goals ahead of your business goals. Only when you clearly identify where you want to go in life can you properly focus your company. It's a necessary shift in perspective that will ensure the company always works for you instead of you working for the company.

## 2. The Milestones or Legs of the Trip

Since the Ultimate Destination is your *personal* vision of success, you must translate these personal goals into the business, and it's at this stage that you figure out where the business needs to go. In Chapter 11 I'll show you how to create a clear and simple business *Scenario* that harnesses your economic engine.

In Chapter 11 I'll also explain how to break the journey down into *legs of the trip* because focusing only on the Ultimate Destination is a fool's ride, as there's lots of road between here and there. The legs are a series of 12- to 18-month milestones your team can wrap their brains around and buy into. By clearly defining the stops along the way, you enable your team to better focus on the right things and ensure a successful journey.

## 3. The Ride Plan or Road Map

Once you've built your Scenario pointing to the first stop on the map, you and your team must figure out the best path to get from here to there. And to do this, you need to build a plan.

However, traditional planning can be painful because we've been taught that a written plan must take days to produce and rival *War and Peace* in size. The end result of this planning is a big honking binder that sits on a shelf and is forgotten after

60 days or so. This is where the *Tactical Planning Process* I describe in Chapter 12 breaks the rules.

It's infinitely more effective than traditional strategic planning and is designed specifically for entrepreneurs who need to move fast. Within a few power-packed hours, you and your team will identify the tactics essential to high performance and success. Once documented, these tactics form a straightforward road map for your business that brings clarity to the day-to-day workings of your organization and turns your vision into reality.

## 4. Communication

Once you've documented the plan, it's all about implementation. Implementation relies on communication, and communication means *meetings*. But let's face it, no one likes to meet.

When I first walk into my client's office and ask questions about the company's meetings, I see eyes begin to roll and hear groans and mutterings about wastes of time. However, there's no way around it. Without meetings, nothing gets done and it's within these meetings that real Navigation takes place.

When held properly, meetings are still the most effective means of communication within any company. In Chapter 14 I'll cover the three types of meetings in business today and explain the components that are crucial to effectively communicating in each.

## 5. Roles and Responsibilities on the Road

You have the plan and you're communicating effectively throughout the organization, but your employees just can't think for themselves and still rely on you to solve all of the problems. By coming to you with every question, they've made you a primary bottleneck while creating a never-ending circle.

Their constant questioning erodes your confidence in their ability to make the right decisions. So you continue to inject yourself into most or all of the decisions, thereby forcing them to continue coming to you because they know you don't trust them. How frustrating is that?

In Chapter 15 I'll show you how to *harness the power of the pack*. I'll explain how using the *Three Ws of Critical Thinking* in Chapter 14 and a few easy-to-implement tools will, over time, stop those pesky little questions and allow you to focus on the big questions. This simple process will remove you from the center of it all, while boosting your confidence in your employees' ability to make the right decisions.

## 6. Riding Skills

Your ability to navigate the gap between *here* and *there* in a timely manner and at a high level of performance depends on *sharpening your skills*.

Accomplished bikers continuously work on their riding skills because they know that the road ahead is ever-changing. Weather conditions, traffic, and other factors beyond their control challenge them each and every time they hit the road, and it's the same in business.

Therefore, the ability of you and your team to both take immediate advantage of opportunities and handle adversity along the way determines the speed at which you reach your goals. And in Chapter 16 I'll share with you the methods I use to develop and sharpen your team's business skills.

Now, drop it into first gear and let's get started because I have some road stories to tell.

 CHAPTER 7

# Finding My Ultimate Destination

*If you don't know where you're going, any road will take you there.*

—Lewis Carroll

One of the things I love most about riding is the solitude it gives you, whether you're riding solo or with others. After all, it's not like you can hold an intelligent conversation with the biker next to you while cruising along at 55 miles per hour. Plus, with a guide leading the way, the only thing I have to worry about is paying attention to the guide's signals and staying between the white lines. This allows my mind to wander—and wander it does.

I'd compartmentalized my thoughts of the past and only focused on the here and now when facing down the cancer. But if I was really going to get a grip on the future, it was time for me to look back and deal with some of the wipeouts of my recent past. And that meant dealing with one whopper in particular.

Now, in my life I've experienced a number of gut-wrenching events that left me gasping for air. Hell, anyone who's lived long enough knows what I'm talking about. But those were usually confined to my personal life, such as the loss of my parents and loved ones and other private issues. However, one of the largest events to blindside me and leave me reeling was also one of the largest in our nation's history: September 11, 2001.

It hit us hard and rocked the entire country. And in addition to the obvious tragedy and terrible loss of life that day, the economic ripple effect felt across the country by businesses everywhere only added to the damage. My own situation turned out to be a rip current that almost took me down and became the catalyst for my business midlife crisis. But before I get into that story, allow me to give you a bit of background information.

In early 1994, fresh out of my career as a turnaround banking guy, I founded my consulting firm. About a year into it, I partnered with an extremely talented friend who had been a top-flight banking executive, and we began to grow quite rapidly. The combination of my expertise in people management and his in finance was a huge advantage for the companies with which we worked.

As our reputation within the entrepreneurial world grew, we were approached by a number of younger companies asking for help. This was during the dot-com boom, and most of the firms seeking assistance were into some really cool technologies. Being classic entrepreneurs and recognizing an opportunity when we saw one, my partner and I soon raised some seed capital and began a fledgling venture company in order to take advantage of this emerging high-tech segment within the central Florida market.

Since we had an enormous amount of business experience in launching companies and assisting entrepreneurs achieve success, our plan was simple: to find a few select companies where our talents best fit, earn some stock, and ride the dot-com wave. Our recruiting efforts proved very successful, and in short order we'd attracted a small stable of emerging technology companies underneath our umbrella.

One of these was run by the ultimate idea guy, who was always chasing three ideas at the same time (something that should have been a huge red flag). The idea that captured our attention was, for its time, a terrific product idea that involved DVDs, sports, and sponsorships. The more we looked into it, the more we liked it, so I hosted a meeting in my living room with the idea guy, my partner, and a dear friend who would become the major investor behind the effort.

As with any start-up venture, there were warning signs and difficulties from the beginning. The first major red flag that I blew by on the project came when we all determined that the idea guy couldn't man the helm to run the business day-to-day. This was when the investor looked across the table at me and said, "I'm in, but Dwain has to run the project." Talk about putting my mouth (or ass) where the money is. It was clear that I had a decision to make.

So a couple of days later—and with no real reason other than the shiny dollar signs gleaming off in the distance—I boldly accepted and off we went. To be fair, I'm not accurately portraying the amount of confidence that I had in the idea at the time; we all believed that this project had tremendous potential, and initial indications were that there would be widespread acceptance. The real problem with my decision became apparent to me when I stopped long enough to realize that I already had a growing company to run full-time. This new side venture meant that I would now be taking my eye off that ball in order to bounce the new one.

To make matters worse, my original partner couldn't take control of the firm, either. His passion as a turnaround guy was taking him off into a totally new direction, where he was already running two other full-time deals. So I made a classic entrepreneurial mistake and turned to one of the longer-termed consultants working with us, thinking that he could take over as president of my firm and run it on a daily basis.

Unsurprisingly, his tenure was short-lived; less than two months later, I asked him to step down due to nonperformance. Lesson learned: It's one thing to work *in* the company, yet quite another to have the balls and passion to lead it. The man I had chosen had neither. This left me running two separate organizations and riding headlong toward an inevitable disaster. Quite predictably, as the new venture began to gain traction and grow, my original company began to slowly lose its way and move in the opposite direction.

Nevertheless, I continued along with the new project. And, in spite of the usual start-up challenges, we found ourselves chasing a significant opportunity with one NFL team, as well as acquiring strong inroads into the NBA and Major League Baseball, a mere nine months after our project's inception. If all worked according to plan, our first paying client would come onboard just as we burned through the funding. But as they say, "The best-laid plans of mice and men . . ." As it turned out, this plan ended in one hell of a "Where were you?" memory—one that burned so deeply into my psyche that it easily comes back as if it were yesterday.

On the morning of September 11, a few business associates and I were in a planning meeting at the offices of our creative design partner, which were located on the back lot of the Disney-MGM Studios in Orlando, Florida. It was a real upbeat morning, as we were putting together the proposal that would, in our minds, win us the first contract on the project. Then, about 45 minutes into our meeting, an executive walked across to our meeting room, opened the door, and yelled that we had to turn on the television set right away.

As we did, I heard my associate—who was sitting next to me and who also worked for a major airline—mutter the word "terrorists" as we watched the second plane slam into the soaring Trade Center tower. From that point on, my colleagues and I, like everyone else that day, sat for what turned into hours in front of the television, rendered speechless and in utter shock. When the first tower fell, I couldn't take any more, and walked outside to get some fresh air and into what can only be described as a parallel universe.

After wandering around and calling a few close friends, I found myself standing less than 100 yards from the Tower of Terror ride, which—since news of the attacks had yet to spread through the park—was still operating. I heard children and adults screaming their lungs out as the ride scared the crap out of them. I began to flinch and tear up, thinking of the real towers of terror being televised live from New York at that moment. It was, in a word, surreal.

I tell this story because something else began to crumble for me that day: everything I'd worked on for the previous nine months of my life. I'd bet the farm on this project, and in one day it was wiped off the table along with so many of my hopes for the future. During one hell of a wake-up call, I found myself perilously close to the abyss that is failure and bankruptcy. Reasonable and controllable risk is one thing, but I'd greatly misjudged the opportunity this time, which left me to metaphorically pick the bits of pavement out of my butt from the wipeout. Having never experienced a terrorist attack on its own soil, the country threw itself into the equivalent of neutral on the transmission of business and dropped the kickstand for a while.

The good news was that no one blamed me for this wipeout, because my business partners were more than understanding.

The major investor, who to this day is my closest friend and confidant, chalked it up to one of those "things that happen" in business, a nothing-ventured, nothing-gained scenario. I could have easily gone along and bought into that state of denial by blaming my venture's collapse on world events beyond my control. I certainly was not alone in feeling the effects of that day; many individuals and companies were in the same spot. But I knew better.

I knew that it was nobody's fault but my own, and my guilt made me feel very alone. I was also gun-shy and began to doubt my ability as a businessperson. The reality was that my failure when this confluence of events occurred was not simply bad luck. I'd needlessly placed myself into a difficult situation and let everyone else down in the process.

In the days and weeks that followed 9/11, my partners and I talked about raising more capital. But these plans ended up going nowhere simply because, in the end, I'd taken a spill from which I just couldn't recover. It was painfully obvious that my heart just wasn't in it anymore; I'd run far afield of my true path, only to get burned for it. In fact, the real lesson that I gleaned from rolling the dice and losing was that my decision-making process was flawed.

It was a brutal realization to discover that any business venture I entered into solely to make money was doomed to certain failure. If I didn't screw it up myself, something else would, because at the first strong wind, that house of cards would most certainly fall. And to make matters worse, I was now returning to a consulting company that was a shell of its former self.

Interestingly enough, as I worked through the emotions of the moment, I felt no anger or remorse over the prospect of being broke, most likely because I'd been there before and this time I was merely close to being broke. My life and career have developed from hard lessons learned on the street; consequently, I always feel dissatisfied with today and focus on tomorrow's mysteries and promise. And the great thing about being broke a time or two over the years is that it not only teaches you how to make money, but gives you a sense of freedom. Like the words of the old Janis Joplin tune, "Freedom's just another word for nothing left to lose," and now I had a pretty clean slate.

I have a healthy determination to win and succeed, which has taken me far beyond my original expectations for life. I tend to think my attitude goes back to growing up in the small Cajun town of Opelousas, Louisiana, where at the tender age of seven I became one of the original latchkey kids, since both of my parents worked. This was not the norm at the time, and I believe that the experience made me extremely independent and self-reliant, traits that have served me well throughout my life.

This autonomous path, along with being a biker, gives me a certain comfort level with risk; I'm inclined to live closer to the edge than most. My willingness to accept risk made me suitable for entrepreneurship, since business owners are usually required to take one leap of faith after another in order to reach the next plateau. But I'm not a gambler in the traditional sense; while gamblers take risks whose outcome depends on chance or outside factors, I take risks in situations that depend more on my personal performance than on factors beyond my control. I've built a career based on understanding how to manage these types of risks, but that's not to say that I haven't had my share of falls. However, each time I've found myself having to get back up, I've merely chalked up the fall to the tuition of life. It has been said that a strength overused becomes a weakness, and the bold determination that had led to my failed venture now had me facing my biggest tuition bill to date.

The reason 9/11 knocked me off my proverbial bike, leaving me dazed and confused on the side of the road, is that the path I'd chosen wasn't *my* path. The dream I'd chased was a collective one, designed by four businessmen sitting in my living room one night. Each contributed their portion of the dream, but I alone wore it like my own suit without ever once considering whether it truly fit me well.

Of all the rough-and-tumble lessons I've learned on this road over the years, this one is by far the most important: When I'm on the path that I know is right for me, I notice that most of the challenges are preceded by doors that don't seem to require major effort to pry open and step through. I don't notice the effort as much when I'm in total harmony with the world; I work my way through these trials, because it's what I'm meant to do. However, because at this point, I hadn't learned this lesson, I rode by each and every road sign along the way to that inevitable crash, never once believing the hazards. I thought that getting a project up and running was *supposed* to be difficult. And where that's certainly true, I'd forgotten the difference between the welcome challenges of your true path and the difficulties of the wrong one.

I desperately needed to get this lesson right before I could possibly look back on it as just another challenge along the way; to do so, I had to strip away the background noise, figure out the message, and determine the right solution. But that caused a dilemma: I had to balance time to think with an essential need to drive revenue. How could I avoid losing everything while ensuring I didn't head off in the wrong direction again?

So there I sat, wondering just what the hell I was going to do next, and this time it meant more than simply getting up, dusting myself off, and jumping back onto the damned bike. It required an attitude that differed greatly from the one I usually employed. Therefore, instead of my normal response of meeting an obstacle with an equal or greater force, I took a Zen approach. Once fully upright and dusted off, I sat quietly but with a purpose.

Some people might consider this to be a passive approach, but that would be dead wrong. In fact, this turned out to be one of the toughest tests I've ever faced. Staying quietly physically as I struggled mentally was enormously difficult; for a person with a highly driven, type A personality, sitting silently for a long period of time is just not a natural state. But there was no other way to dig deep within myself to determine just who I was in this world of business and figure out exactly where I fit in.

I also reminded myself that the majority of my poor decisions came when I acted too quickly and ended up gaining false momentum. So I stopped the ride in order to see what flowed to me naturally. I asked myself: What would grow in my life if I didn't actively make it rain? What types of business opportunities would all of my hard work over the years—along with my background, reputation, and abilities—naturally attract? Making this discovery, however, was merely one part of the answer. The solution as a whole lay beyond honing my ability to make money and involved figuring out *why* I'd wanted to do so in the first place. I needed to understand what direction I wanted to go in once the business started coming in.

The breakthrough came on a series of sunny afternoons when I rode out to another friend's boathouse and sat on the dock feeling the serenity that water brings. I sat alone with my trusty yellow pad for hours, thinking hard about my business, my life, or nothing at all. I eventually took a page from Jim Collins' outstanding book *Good to Great* (Collins Business, 2001) and worked on my own personal Hedgehog Concept. For those of you unfamiliar with this theory, it boils down to three simple questions: First, what are you absolutely passionate about? Second, what can you be the best at in the world? And third, will people pay you for it?

I began to list everything I loved to do in business on my pad, and I kept it simple. If it was something I'd leave my sickbed to do, that meant I *loved* it; if it wasn't, it didn't make the list. This was the criteria I would use as the natural business flow brought more and more opportunities my way. What I discovered as I made my list was that I truly love being a Navigator of companies, since it's a role that embodies all of my talents. Now I simply had to structure my company in such a way that I could focus solely on that aspect of business. Unfortunately, the current structure of the company presented me with many things I didn't want to do—which left me to begin sorting those out.

I continued my self-assessment, and on one page I listed everything necessary to rebuild the type of company that I truly wanted. Then on a separate page, using an old-fashioned T account, I broke that list down into two sections. One side listed the things I loved about running the company, and the other listed the things I hated about running the company.

It was the list of things on the right-hand side of that T account—the tasks I disliked—that I needed to either get rid of or accept. I had a moment of clarity when looking at the list, one that shifted my world as I realized how my vision had been influenced by others. It was time to take the lessons I'd learned and create my own way. It was time to be true to *myself*.

I didn't have a college degree, but my street-level education had provided me with confidence and determination in most areas. However, it had also left me lacking in others, which had made me far too susceptible to the ideas of those I considered more accomplished than me. Until now, I'd placed too much value on their opinions about my direction and how I went about getting there. I came to understand that it's one thing to receive advice; it's yet another to allow this well-meaning feedback to rule your path. As my biking instructor told me, "Just because the rider in front of you takes the curve at 65 miles per hour or goes down a certain road, doesn't mean that you have to. You have to trust your own abilities and instincts." While some bikers feel that it's all about speed and daring, successful ones know that it's really about riding within your abilities and desires.

Early on in business, I equated success with building a bigger organization, since companies tend to be measured by size rather than content. Like most entrepreneurs and business leaders, I became growth driven at all costs. During that quest for success, I forgot to build the company in a way that works for *me*—not the other way around! And in doing so, I almost lost my soul. I got caught up in the trap of thinking, "If it has that much potential, then in order for the world to consider me a success, I *have* to reach it!" It was time to stop listening to all of the well-meaning advisors out there telling me that I should do business this way or that. I needed to believe in myself, saddle up, and ride the damn bike *my* way.

You'll never hear an experienced biker planning a day- or week-long ride say something like, "The fastest way to my destination is this way, so let's bust our butts to get there in record time." Hell no! The biker instead asks what route offers the greatest experience and most rewarding ride. It was now time to listen to my inner biker in order to determine which business route offered me the most satisfaction. If my vision of success conflicted with what others perceived as the company's potential size and scope—whatever the hell that was—then so be it. After all, it was my company, and if I couldn't find the sweet spot between the company's potential and achieving my vision of personal success, then the chances of reaching either were slim.

I realized, therefore, that it was more important for me to build a great organization that affected my business community in a unique and significant way than it was to form a big company. I knew with crystal-clear certainty that in order to achieve this new vision of success, I needed to take only those actions that held true to my mission.

Fast forward five years—and I'm now sitting on the side of a mountain, looking down onto cloud-covered peaks. The question now is not how to build a great company (as I had contemplated at the lake house years earlier) but how to take this great company I've built and fuel a great life while achieving the ultimate win–win.

After communing with the clouds, I saddled up and began to ride. I now needed to go back and repeat the process that, years ago, had brought me successfully to this point. I needed to ask myself *The Question*:

> *It's five years from now and my entire life has gone according to plan—every challenge overcome, every goal achieved. What does it look like?*

This is by no means an easy question to answer. In fact, it's getting tougher all the time because of the rate at which things are moving around us today. But I needed to take the time necessary to think about and answer that question because I knew it would help me to find the balance between my work and my life.

A lot of people talk in terms of achieving balance; it seems to be one of life's most coveted yet elusive goals. In the early days of my company, I went to a speech given by business management writer Tom Peters. Midway through the lecture, he began to discuss the issue of life balance. The example he used was from the Atlanta Olympics, which was taking place at that time. He talked about how each of the teenage girls on the balance beam awakened every morning before dawn, went to practice, and then returned home to shower and head off to school. After school they spent more time training and then returned home to do their homework, have dinner, and go to sleep.

The girls did this every day. They didn't go to parties, weren't in the school play, and didn't hang out at the movies with their friends. Their lives, as viewed by the average person, were totally out of balance. Until you dropped in one little factor—*they were going for gold!* Once you included that piece of information, you saw that the girls were in total balance, because they'd each identified and bought into their finish line.

Every one of our lives is filled with gold medal moments. The trouble is that, as entrepreneurs, we often lose sight of the finish lines. In the early days, we had to work 70 hours a week to make it, but once we've achieved a level of success, we forget to turn off the "always going" mentality. We've long ago blown past our original gold medal moment and replaced it with a new one without recalibrating the effort necessary to achieve it. To return to the Olympics analogy, after winning gold at the Olympics, the gymnast would not continue training like mad if her goal was now to get a college degree. She would reassess her situation and determine what it would take to reach her new goal.

I did this reassessment myself, and I know that I no longer want to go full-out and work 60 to 70 hours a week to simply grow my company. I want to work a saner schedule, smell the roses along the way, and stop at a few roadside attractions by taking a few long weekends or a couple of weeks off. I want to have a damned life outside of the company, and that's OK! After all, it's my company; I went into this not to prove anything to anybody else, but to create and control my life's journey. Therefore, I now needed to take the rest of this road trip and come up with my answer. I also needed to put it out there for the universe to see and act upon—because that creates momentum. Once all is said and done, it's my ride—it's where I want and need to go.

**Road Rules**

- It's imperative that you look at your life and business in total.
- Look beyond next week, next month, or next year—you must go out three to five years.
- Use The Question to determine what you really want out of life.
- It's OK to be selfish, because if you're not taking care of your own needs, you will not be able to take care of the needs of others.

*You can access my free tools to help you find your Ultimate Destination, along with detailed instructions, on my Web site at www.BikersGuidetoBusiness.com.*

CHAPTER 8

# It's My Ride

After 9/11 crushed the project I'd been working on, I spent a lot of time both alone with my thoughts and seeking advice from my closest friends and confidants. At that time, two of these people were my partners in the consulting firm. While one worked with me on a daily basis, the other lived across the state and served as more of a mentor than an active partner.

During the time that I spent on the project, my local partner began to follow his emerging path in the world of turnarounds, a position to which he's perfectly suited. For me, this further highlighted the fact that our venture project was at a fork in the road—at which he was taking one path and I was taking the other.

The funny thing about coming to a crossroads like that is that in the beginning, you start down your respective paths still able to see, touch, and hear each other. As you continue to travel these paths, you quickly lose physical touch while still seeing and hearing each other. A little farther along, you can no longer see the other person, but you can still hear him. You eventually lose that as well, though, when the mountain comes between you. Now two questions arise: Are you simply going around and meeting on the other side? Or are you heading off in totally separate directions, never to connect again? In the case of my partners and me, it turned out to be both.

The seminal moment came late one afternoon in October as we met—for the last time as partners—in my living room. We needed to discuss the option that my inactive partner had proposed a few weeks earlier: selling the company and all of its intellectual property to someone who wanted to flee New York after the tragedy. On the surface, it was a viable option, but I had to think about it.

In the two weeks leading up to the meeting, I'd decided, as I mentioned earlier, to lie low in order to see what naturally grew around me if I didn't "make it rain." So instead of running around, frantically trying to drum up business as usual, I spent time sitting and thinking at my friend's boathouse. I desperately needed to clear my head in order to gain enough clarity to answer *The Question*.

*The Question* is a self-assessment, goal-setting tool. As I mentioned in Chapter 7, it allows me to wrap my mind around an all-important question: What do I want my life to look like five years into the future? And so I quietly sat on that dock to try to figure this out. I spent hours on end, day after day, pondering an outline filled with my thoughts and compiling a separate list of business dos and don'ts.

To make the process even more difficult, I was pretty much down and out financially, so in between my thinking times at the boathouse, I did the odd consulting project. These sporadic gigs provided some much-needed revenue and helped me to gain some focus. They allowed me to earn money while working on my answer to *The Question* and served as a litmus test for my list of business dos and don'ts. If what I was working on lit up my senses, I put it in the "do" column. If it didn't, it went into the "don't" column.

This course of action led to my inevitable decision *not* to sell my firm, because navigating companies is what I really wanted to do. One might say that I wasted time on an obvious answer, but the real value came in identifying the changes I needed to make not only to get the company back on track, but to fuel my passions as well. Giving myself a deadline of two weeks was also helpful because it forced me to make my decision the day before I was scheduled to meet with my two partners.

The meeting began with my inactive partner eulogizing the organization. She talked about the many companies that I and my Navigation Process had helped over the years. We discussed the many entrepreneurs who had reaped the benefits of our services and lamented the fact that it would be a shame to see the company go. At that point I smiled and said, "Glad you both agree, because I've decided to keep the company."

What happened next was not a complete surprise, but it was close. My inactive partner launched into a recitation of my past sins as a businessman and leader (how I ran my first company), and said that I was blowing my only chance to get out of my current hole. That blow sent me reeling. What I had wanted and expected most at that moment from a supposed partner was support, not a kick in the head. It was obvious that she'd already made the decision to walk away from the company, and that I was simply not listening to reason.

To his credit, my other partner didn't pile on the criticism. He did, however, explain why he wouldn't be an active part of the company's resurrection. It was clear that his focus was on the turnaround area of the business world, and that two clients were taking up his schedule full-time. And while I certainly appreciated his position and candor, I'd never felt so alone. These were my partners; one was berating my incompetence, while the other was simply leaving. I was so upset that I could no longer even hear what they were saying, and had the overwhelming feeling that they couldn't leave my house soon enough.

What I realized later that evening was that, in addition to the sting of personal loss I'd suffered earlier that day, I'd also experienced a tremendous epiphany. I realized that in their eyes, the company was nothing more than an economic engine. One partner saw it as a passive investment that would pay a dividend some day, while the other had used it as a vehicle to launch his career in another direction. Neither was *wrong* in their view of the business; they simply didn't have the emotional attachment to it that I did.

That painful but vitally important encounter taught me that at the end of the day, only one person will truly buy into a company's vision, and that's the founder. The other people will ride along as long as they're taken care of and can fit the company into their personal agendas. Again, there's nothing morally wrong with that reality, but I picked one hell of a tough way to learn it.

After my two partners finally left, I did what I normally do under such frustrating circumstances. I sat quietly on my patio for hours searching for the deeper lesson while pondering my business future—alone. While sitting there, I realized that their leaving would force me to trust in my own vision and free me to build the company my way. I no longer needed anyone's approval, nor would I ever again allow someone to alter my plans. The age-old saying "In the future, if it is to be, it's up to me" rang loudly through my brain.

When the sunlight faded to black, I walked into the empty house and found a little stroke of destiny that hit the evening like a mountain road switchback and turned the entire night around. On the table, still in its bag, was the book I'd purchased earlier that day on how to build a top-flight consulting business. And so I sat down with a very large glass of wine and began to read it.

Chapter after chapter, as the author described what I needed to think about and do, I began to mentally say, "Check, I've got that . . . Check, done that, too." After much wine, I managed to finish the book, and along the way I realized that everything I needed was, astonishingly, *already in place*. Sure, it needed a tweak here and there, but essentially I was good to go. With that thought in mind, I slept like a baby (I'm sure the wine helped, too). I awoke the next day focused and energized about my future. I was ready to go.

And think about it—isn't that always the case? When faced with a major obstacle or perceived failure, the first thing we do is doubt ourselves and reach out to others who, in our eyes, know more and are wiser than us. But are they *really*? I needed to remember that the main difference at that moment between myself and my two ex-partners was that I was the one—as my inactive partner had so bluntly put it—"in the ditch." And their frame of reference, though valuable, was theirs alone. It was comprised solely of *their* experiences, fears, and drivers, and these no longer matched my own.

This was my lesson! This fallout with my partners was the wipeout that commanded my attention; I'd used my fall to see my current predicament from a different direction and gain incredible clarity. I needed to remember that in the end, everything to this point was my experience and mine alone. There was no way for them to fully understand what I'd learned while sitting out on that boat dock. Taking that time had allowed me to prevent their opinions from creating fear and causing me to doubt my chosen path. I knew for sure that it was always *my ride* and there was nothing left to do but keep on going.

 CHAPTER 9

# Meeting Life at the Crossroads

It was just after seven o'clock in the morning on July 4, and the cold air greeted me as I stepped out of the Delaware Hotel in the mountains of Colorado and climbed onto my Road King. I was three days into a seven-day ride through the stunning high country of Colorado on a journey to celebrate life. It wasn't a milestone birthday or a trip to commemorate any kind of business achievement. This ride was part of my attempt to work through the wake-up call I'd received less than two years earlier—when a surgeon successfully removed my left kidney due to a cancerous tumor.

Y'know, there's nothing quite like the feeling I got when the doctor looked me in the eye and dropped that damned C word. In fact, that's the only thing from that entire conversation that I can remember him saying, because for the next 15 minutes, nothing else registered. There I sat, in the prime of life, staring mortality in the face and thinking, "Crap, another fight." Only this time, it was for my life.

I wrote earlier that there are two types of riders in this world: those who have laid their bikes down, and those that will. This has also been a metaphor for my life in general; I've experienced my share of wipeouts and overcome a few obstacles along my journey. I learned at the tender age of 17 what it was like to pick myself up off the pavement and get back on the bike after meeting the wrong end of a '65 Ford. That single accident forced me to spend the entire summer between my junior and senior years of high school in partial traction nursing a few broken bones.

And of course, I had learned that same hard lesson in business—more than once. Between the struggles following 9/11 and the sheer sense of isolation, albeit brief, that I felt when my partners and I went our separate ways, I knew what it was to hit the ground hard. But as I discovered when I got back onto that bike my senior year, wipeouts in business are a fact of life and any entrepreneur worth his or her salt has also laid it down a time or two on the road to success.

This time, however, was enormously different. This wasn't just a setback or relatively normal life event that one simply overcomes. For me, contracting cancer just shy of turning the Big 5-0 was the biggest, most badass thing I'd ever faced, and it caused all kinds of clutter to invade my head. This cancer thing seriously staggered me, and I needed to regain my life balance before laying it down for good.

Many of the incredible cancer survivors with whom I spoke with after receiving my diagnosis cautioned me against wasting my time and energy by focusing on the past and wondering what, if anything, I'd do over, as that was out of my control and irrelevant. Once I survived, I could face those demons of the past—and I did. One particular survivor who had an especially profound impact was younger than me, had a family, and said that he spent his time focusing more on them than on himself. He told me that not only was it important for him to enjoy being with them each and every day, but it was also imperative that he teach them how to enjoy *him* each and every day. He warned me—and my own experience later confirmed his words—that once your friends and family learn about the disease, they begin to see and treat you differently. Some will no longer come around out of fear of "getting in the way," while others are simply afraid to be around illness.

But this new friend of mine stressed that the world around me would react according to the way *I* acted, and that my attitude and actions needed to be honest, real, and not hollow. That is why, when facing this disease, it's important to only concentrate on the here and now of the struggle. Luckily for me, this was not a problem as my life has been filled with ups and downs. So, as I had done with so many of life's previous challenges, I totally focused on understanding the disease and how to beat it.

The mere word *cancer* conjured up all sorts of fears and bad memories for me, because it's a disease with which my family has an extensive and unfortunate history. My mother died of colon cancer at the "too young to die" age of 58, mainly because she refused to listen to her body and was too afraid of the news she'd receive when going to the doctor. Unfortunately, by the time she *did* go, the disease had progressed to the point where nothing could be done, and she passed away within six weeks of her diagnosis. Though incredibly painful, that experience taught me the importance of early diagnosis and information. That is why, two weeks into my symptoms of intense fatigue, I went to my doctor and began running the battery of tests that eventually revealed the malignant tumor.

Once the diagnosis was confirmed, the business side of my brain kicked in. Early in my career, I had learned to always run to a problem with open eyes and an open mind—and that is what I did. I was lucky to live in a time when so much information was available through the click of a mouse, and I spent hours online, reading many of the hundreds of stories about others who had faced this challenge and lived through it. I looked up information on aftercare and nutritional needs going forward. I was also blessed to have a dear friend who is a doctor; she spent a great deal of time translating the medical speak I encountered on a regular basis, so that I could understand what I was dealing with.

I'm happy to report that with the help of an excellent surgeon and his medical team, I made it through. Minus one kidney, I had a good prognosis; a full recovery was expected and the cancer was thankfully gone. All that was left was for me to weave my way through the mental minefield that comes from a brush with death.

The Big C rudely reminded me that time has a way of flying by much too quickly and the full-length feature that is my life could, at any time, come to an abrupt end. The questions were coming at me fast and furious and beginning to freak me out. How much time before the next bullet and will it get me? Is my life heading in the right direction? What should I do now and why? Is it all really worth it? Should I hurry or continue to cruise along like before? Hell, do I *really* know what happiness is?

All good questions, because in the end life is about enjoying the ride, and so it was crucial that I figure out the answers. This time I was lucky to have dodged the endgame, but we all know that life is temporary. I wasn't necessarily near the end of my life's movie, but this incident showed me that the end credits to the film were clearly standing by in the queue.

To put it another way, I was sitting at the crossroads of business and life, desperately needing to mentally pick myself up off the pavement one more time. I urgently needed to refocus my passions and figure out where I really wanted to go in life. In biker speak, I had to get my shit together because I just might be running out of do-over time.

I thought about how to do that, and I actually ended up taking my own advice, which I've given to clients who've come to similar crossroads. I've come to call them Generation Next. These seasoned entrepreneurs and business leaders have achieved a level of success in their business life, are still relatively young, and now find themselves looking down from the mountaintop and asking, "What's next?"

That's a tricky place to be, because up until this point, their lives have been pretty clear in terms of goals and vision. They've successfully crossed the finish lines they set when starting out and now need to establish some new ones. In working through this, I counsel them that it takes serious quiet time to get their thoughts in order, which usually requires extended time off from work.

But for me and most other entrepreneurs, a vacation from my business was a foreign concept. Real time away was always something I figured that I'd get to *someday,* yet now that day had arrived in a not-so-subtle fashion. And this soul searching certainly wasn't something I could accomplish over a four-day weekend or my typical Wednesday-to-Wednesday week off. No, it needed to be a significant amount of time, and of course, it needed to involve a big ride.

I always turn to my bike when I need to clear my head in order to do some serious thinking, because riding is my quiet time, my Zen retreat, the oasis where I go to reflect. I can't think about too many things at once when I'm on the bike, simply because I have to pay attention to the ride. At the beginning, my senses are always totally in the moment—until I get into the groove and onto some backcountry road where it's just me, the wind, birds, and smells.

But this time I needed to leave the familiar countryside of Florida and the East Coast and ride in a part of the country where I could totally lose myself in order to find my true path. I'm not sure why, but the first place to pop into my mind was Colorado. Probably because I've always loved the mountains, having skied them over the years, but I'd never ridden through them. So after a bit of research, I selected the High Road Tour. Led by a marvelous husband and wife team, participants spend the week riding from one mountain town to another, never sleeping in the same place twice. In addition to the pleasure of having no routine for the week, I got really lucky and turned out to be the only rider. That made the week perfect in that there was a minimum of human contact, giving me much-needed solitude both on and off the bike.

And so here I was, saddling up to leave the supercool old mining town of Leadville, where we'd spent the previous night. Atop a mountain, it's the highest incorporated city in North America and nicknamed Cloud City because it sits at 10,430 feet above sea level. The sunset was an awesome sight; I watched the sky turn purplish red as the clouds rose to hide both the sun and the snow-covered peaks in the distance. God's Country, to be sure.

Leadville turned out to be my favorite town of the week because of its history and character. Little about the town or its architecture has changed since it was founded in 1877. In its heyday, Leadville hosted such noted characters as Doc Holliday, Buffalo Bill, and even Oscar Wilde, making it an easy mental leap for me to pretend that I was back in time mounting a real horse, rather than the iron one underneath me. Once I got on, my guide, Tom, and I began another meandering ride that would eventually end that afternoon in a town called Steamboat Springs.

Just as the sun burned away the morning's mist, I noticed that each day's ride gently burned away the distractions wandering through my head. As we wound our way through the still-empty streets lined with red, white, and blue bunting that awaited the crowds to come later that day, I no longer felt guilty about leaving the business behind. The ride was now working as the sights, smells, and sounds of the Colorado countryside relaxed me and cleared my mind.

And then approximately two miles outside of town, we topped a mountain at over 11,000 feet and I literally *rode through a cloud!* That was a first for me and the wet, crisp mountain air brought a tear to my eye and a shiver to my spine, rocking me with a moment of intense clarity. It was as if the universe had given me this huge hug, and it's the type of breakthrough experience that only riding a motorcycle can bring. You may see this from the front seat of a car, but you *feel* it when on a bike.

Once I broke through the cloud back into the bright sunshine, I stopped and got off my bike to look down onto the cloud and snap a picture of it and the mountainside below. I then sat there taking in that incredible view and began to feel as if the cloud had stripped me of all life connections and instantly wiped my slate clean. It was forcing me to look beyond my routine need to achieve and to look at my life in total. I knew then that this ride wasn't just about figuring out which new road to take. Instead, this new crossroads I'd come to was forcing me to question my entire direction and purpose in life.

I realized that, somewhere along the line, my perspective on why I do what I do had been lost. Almost a decade and half earlier, I had launched my own business to control my destiny and achieve the lifestyle I dreamed of. But somehow, the business had begun to own *me*. Yes, from a basic life perspective, I'd achieved security and a reasonable level of success, but what next? How could I make sure that, going forward, I wasn't simply doing what I *had* to do, but was also doing what I *wanted* to do?

It was so much easier in the early days to figure that kind of stuff out. My mission was much more fundamental back then; it had as much to do with just surviving another day as it did with growing. Sheer passion and my "do what it takes" attitude drove my relentless aspirations for years. However, I now faced an awakening in life that required a different approach. My circumstances had shifted drastically, and developing my company was no longer my number one motivation in life—simply *living* life was!

Problem is, over the years, as my business grew and I began to prosper financially, I gradually began to accept that my personal needs and desires would take a back seat. I continued to focus daily on what the company needed, and I was more concerned about *its* direction than my own. For me, success depended on the ability to harness and direct my passion. It was easy to remain focused on the company; that's where my passions lay. So, like most entrepreneurs, I found it easier to concentrate on the business side of success than on the personal, because trying to do both got too complicated.

Hell, ask me where my company needs to be in five years, and I'll answer without a moment's hesitation. However, ask me where I want *my life* to be in five years, and I couldn't begin to tell you. And after all these years in business, that's a pretty crappy place to be. I'd allowed the needs of the company to drive my personal life for too long. It was high time to answer the question "What's next?" and redefine my dreams. It was time to focus on my *lifestyle*.

To do that, I needed to stop and identify and confirm my personal goals, because the place I was heading might not be the right direction. What *really* ticked me off was the moment of almost stupidly clear self-awareness that hit me after riding through that damned cloud. I was suddenly and rudely reminded that I'd fallen into the same trap that I'd helped my clients get out of on a daily basis. I saw the same warning signs in others and helped them work through it every single day, yet managed to totally miss the same signals in my own life. In fact, I'd just become the frigging cliché of the master motorcycle mechanic whose own bike is always the last to be repaired.

And so, right there on the spot, I decided to spend the rest of the ride applying to my very own life the tools and processes I've honed over the years by helping others navigate their situations. And that, in a nutshell, is what this book is about. It's a guide on how to look at yourself in the mirror and ask some very difficult questions—one, in particular, is the topic of the entire next chapter. Once you've managed to answer *The Question*, I'll discuss in more detail how you can apply my straightforward process to identify the "who," "what," and "how" that are necessary to get there. This process isn't just about or for bikers; it's merely the lessons learned by *this* biker in successfully navigating through the same crossroads of business and life that thousands of other entrepreneurs reach each and every day.

And like any road trip, it begins by lifting the kickstand and shifting gears. So saddle up, and let's ride.

 CHAPTER 10

# Figuring It Out

On the surface, *The Question* looks simple enough, but it's actually loaded with tremendous uncertainty, as the road is wide and unclear. When asking this question of my clients for the first time, their immediate response is usually a blank stare followed by, "I don't know ... Hell, I can barely see beyond next month!" *The Question* is a bit unfair. It's almost impossible to answer that inquiry off the top of your head until you spend some time thinking about the future. But the issue is always how to properly do this.

The funny thing about this is although I've used this tool to assist my clients over the years, I'd never really used it myself—that is, until that time after 9/11. When I finally did face *The Question*, I struggled mightily with it. It was then that I created The Questionnaire (detailed in this chapter) with the help of my clients. This simple four-page survey helped me to first wrap my head around where I am today, and also helped me gauge where it was that I really wanted to be in the future. This exercise challenged me to think about my business and personal side of life in tandem, so that I could more effectively identify the conflicts and trade-offs that I needed to deal with in order to move forward.

In order to work through the questions properly, I needed to take my good sweet time, because this wasn't just homework—it was about my future. I needed to carve out an hour or two of uninterrupted time for better idea flow, and what better way to do that than on the back of my bike riding across Colorado? It didn't take long for me to begin pondering the big questions, and with the aid of my trusty digital recorder, document my answers at each rest and fuel stop.

## Part 1: Present Personal Vision

I always insist that you begin by putting your personal life first, because this is the part that, surprisingly, tends to take the most thought. We're entrepreneurs, and as such, we are programmed to think primarily about business. Therefore, putting your personal interests first sends a subliminal signal to your brain that things are going to be different. You also avoid inadvertently blocking important life goals by having the business overshadow your thinking.

---

### Personal Vision

#### Present

**My favorite ways to spend time:**

_____

_____

_____

_____

_____

_____

**The most important people in my life:**

_____

_____

_____

_____

_____

_____

**My greatest past learning experiences:**
**(physical, mental, spiritual, social)**

_____

_____

_____

_____

_____

**My greatest "hits" and accomplishments:**

_____

_____

_____

_____

_____

**My greatest challenges:**

_____

_____

_____

_____

_____

So the first question I asked myself was, *What are my favorite ways to spend time?*

This was a tough one for me, because I like to do *a lot* of stuff! Of course, I was supposed to narrow it down to my *favorite* activities, so my list included items like spending time with my family, riding my bike, cooking, entertaining my friends, reading, and smoking a great cigar. It's really easy here to mix business and personal, so remember, this is strictly personal. You'll get to business later.

The next question I dealt with was, *Who are the most important people in my life?*

The reasoning behind this question is easy; these are the people who have a tremendous influence on your world, both today and in the future. Any decision you make going forward will certainly affect them as well.

Besides, few people ride alongside us our entire lives and my own history is filled with great people who have come and gone. Each of us rolls down our own path and it's important to recognize sooner rather than later where our paths begin to diverge, so we're not counting on someone at a time when they can no longer deliver. Plus it's always interesting to see who makes the cut, who doesn't, and why.

The key here is not to take the why of it all personally and let it bug you as I did for years. Indeed, parting ways with some people is painful, but I've learned over time that who walks away from whom isn't the issue. If you only focus on the parting, you'll miss the lesson and the reason why you were brought together in the first place. Or to put it another way, no ride lasts forever, so enjoy and experience those around you while it's happening.

I then reflected on *my greatest past learning experiences.*

I took into account my physical, mental, spiritual, and social experiences. I listed lessons learned on the back of the bike (of course), what I learned about myself from the surgery and the associated spiritual awakening, and so on. For me, making this list always gives me one or two "Aha!" moments. I usually recall something that I glossed over long ago, but that's extremely important in shaping the individual I am today.

Next I segued right into *my greatest hits or accomplishments.*

I always love this mental pat on the back, because this is no time for being humble. I listed them all and smiled as I looked back on the good work I've done. It's an important thing to stop and allow yourself to be proud once in a while.

And to ensure that it didn't go to my head, I quickly balanced my thinking by then acknowledging *my greatest challenges.*

Although I use the word *challenges* here, I really mean screwups, mistakes, and major FUBARs. I listed them all and did my best not to go into a funk, all the while reminding myself that they are all just learning experiences in life and must be treated as such. Thankfully, this list wasn't longer than my list of accomplishments. If it had been, well, it wouldn't have been pretty.

## Part 2: Future Personal Vision

Next I began thinking about the future of my personal life. In other words, it was time to dream about all those things I'd always wanted to do but hadn't gotten around to. It was time to make them a priority, and the following set of questions helped me figure out how.

---

### Personal Vision

**Future**

**Someday I would like to:**

_____

_____

_____

_____

_____

*(continued)*

---

**People I want to know:**

_____

_____

_____

_____

_____

_____

**New learning experiences:**
**(physical, mental, spiritual, social)**

_____

_____

_____

_____

_____

**Future accomplishments:**

_____

_____

_____

_____

_____

**Future challenges:**

_____

_____

_____

_____

_____

The first question I pondered was, *Someday I would like to _____.*

The answers to this one flowed easily; I had a mile-long list of things I wanted to do in my life. I wanted to ride my motorcycle across the United States, Canada, Europe, and Australia. Throw in a bit of snow skiing, boating with friends, and a few select blues festivals and art shows, and I was just getting started. I won't bore you with further details, but you get the point. It doesn't matter how impossible you think these goals might be; list them anyway. If you want to do it, it goes on the list.

I found the next one interesting: *people I want to know.*

This was simply a chance to list people I wanted to know better and who I believed would enrich my world. I really got into that whole "six degrees of separation" thing and imagined myself hanging out backstage with ZZ Top or riding with really cool people like Bob Parsons, CEO of GoDaddy.Com and Phil Jackson, coach of the Lakers. The interesting thing is that no matter how creative I get with this list, I can usually find a way to meet them, and believe it or not, you can, too.

In my recent travels I've met Tom Peters, hung out with Dan Aykroyd at a Canadian blues fest, and rode with the likes of John Paul DeJoria and Bob Parsons. Some meetings have been planned while others were happenstance. In either case, it begins by putting yourself out there and grabbing the opportunity when it presents itself.

The third question on the list had to do with *new learning experiences.*

One of the keys to my success is that I've always been a lifelong learner, so this is where I was able to focus on my overall development. I considered some areas that I wanted to work on and thought about the new things I wanted to discover. I took into account factors like my weight and overall health, new conferences I wanted to attend, or classes I wanted to take.

I also thought about new ideas in the area of spirituality that I might want to explore.

This led into the list of *my future accomplishments.*

*Now* it was goal setting time, the time to be aggressive in terms of deciding what I wanted to accomplish going forward. The thing to remember here is not to limit yourself when it comes to time. Remember, these should be things that you want to do within the context of the next five years. So I went for it, and listed as many goals as I thought were possible. After all, it's always better to shoot for 10 things and hit 8, than go for 6 and hit 3.

My last task in the personal section was to identify *my future challenges.*

I quickly identified the known challenges, such as home improvements and my family's needs, and tried to anticipate when I would need to address them. When you consider your challenges, include whatever you can think of that will cause you to change your focus during the next five years. I know that it's impossible to see every challenge that's lurking out there in the future, but if life's taught me one thing, it's that we all have them coming—and it's good to be prepared.

Thinking through those personal questions didn't distract me one bit from the mountain scenery. If anything, the incredible backdrop of rolling high meadows and wide open pastureland ensured that I kept my mind wide open as well. I was feeling good about what I'd accomplished along the way and knew from past experience that if I'd missed anything, I'd just add it when transcribing my digitally recorded thoughts onto paper, and if I'd included things that didn't belong, I'd just omit them. The good news was I had the gist of it done and in the can.

Next it would be time to think about business, but before I did that, I decided to simply let my mind wander instead. I find that trying to focus on the entire Questionnaire in a single sitting is counterproductive, so I put it aside for the time being and just enjoyed the scenery the rest of the way into Steamboat. After all, it was July 4 and a time to celebrate.

Good thing I didn't let the questions distract me, because the route we took on this leg of the trip was especially spectacular. We crossed the Continental Divide at Tennessee Pass and then visited Camp Hale, where the 10th Mountain Division—the ski troops—trained during World War II. We then rolled over the Vail Pass into Dillon, through the town of Kremmling, and across the Gore Pass.

That evening we enjoyed a terrific fireworks show, great food, and cold beer. And after a good night's sleep, I awoke at my customary East Coast time; it wasn't quite dawn yet in the mountains. I brewed a cup of coffee and sat out on the porch enjoying the crisp, fresh air and mountain scenery. As I sat there e-mailing a few friends, I began to hear something that sounded like a thruster revving up. It was two hot air balloons coming to life. One was striped in green, blue, gold, and red with "Wild West" stenciled on it, while the other was striped in green, purple, gold, and red with a huge Batman symbol. I thought how cool it would be to take a ride in one of them and wished I'd known about that possibility in advance, because it would have been kick-ass to see the view from up there.

That said, my vantage point on the bike so far hadn't been too bad either; this mountain tour was hovering in the awesome zone. It was a glorious trip. At times, we rolled down back roads so deserted that the only things we passed for miles were moose and deer. It left me really looking forward to the next leg of the trip at the end of each day.

After a lazy morning's breakfast, we packed up and rolled south on Highway 40, eventually cruising through Rabbit Ears Pass at 9,426 feet, crossing the Continental Divide again, and then turning northeast toward Walden. We passed a couple more moose on our way to the top of Cameron Pass and then headed back into Walden for lunch at this cool-as-can-be restaurant with antlers everywhere.

After lunch, I turned my attention to the business side of life, while we rolled across the Continental Divide for the second time at the Willow Creek Pass on our way to Granby, and eventually down the Frasier River Valley. I decided that it was time to answer the questions about my professional life that I had so thoughtfully addressed for my personal life.

## Part 3: Present Business Vision

The first thing that I did was to think about my present situation. This would serve as a baseline, which I needed to establish in order to move forward in a new direction.

---

### Business Vision

#### Present

**My role:**

_____

_____

_____

_____

_____

**What I like about my role:**

_____

_____

_____

_____

_____

---

**Key people/positions:**

_____

_____

_____

_____

_____

**Most important learning experience:**

_____

_____

_____

_____

_____

**Greatest accomplishments:**

_____

_____

_____

_____

_____

So I started by considering *my current role.*

It was immediately obvious to me that I filled more than just one role; I listed everything that was currently required of me in my business. I was president, Navigator, coach, mentor, trusted advisor, accounts payable clerk, marketer, and salesman. As you can tell by my list, mine is a small company and I wear many hats, but that's pretty universal in most entrepreneurial organizations. I've seen positions like janitor, maintenance man, and the like when I've helped my clients establish their lists. Don't worry if you forget to name everything. You can always add to it later.

Next came the fun part: *what I like about my role.*

I broke down the list I had just made, but didn't make anything up. In other words, I didn't pretend to enjoy a task that I found unbearable. For instance, I *hated* paying bills, so I said nothing about that. On the flip side, I loved everything about navigating, so I created quite a list about that. It's important to go with your emotions here, and be as honest as possible about why you enjoy a certain role. You need to put it all on the table.

Next I looked at the entire organization to list the *key people and key positions.*

Who were the people playing a crucial part in the organization? Since I was involved in several different ventures, I had a number of outside resources and strategic partners that I recorded in this portion of the list: my designer, printer, accountant, and others. To determine who was vital, I asked myself which people I would *least* want to lose, and which positions I would *not* want to do without.

Just a hint: You might have a problem if there's a key position listed and the person manning it didn't show up on your key person list. That should certainly give you pause!

Now I turned my attention to *my most important learning experience.*

Just as I had done with the personal side of my life, I looked back at the times—both good and bad—that taught me the lessons that brought me to this level. I listed conferences, classes, my business coach, and yes, those tough "fall on my face" lessons, although thinking about these was not always pleasant.

But I then I offset any tough lessons with the next list: *my greatest accomplishments.*

The clients I'd recruited, ventures I'd launched, articles I'd published, and speeches I'd given, as well as the community organizations I'd helped along the way, were all included on this list. I also added items like mentoring an employee or winning an award. As I mentioned before, patting myself on the back is something I, and most other people, rarely do, so it's nice to take the time to recognize and applaud your own efforts once in a while.

## Part 4: Future Business Vision

Now that I'd documented the baseline of the important segments of my business, it was goal-setting time once again. As in the personal section of The Questionnaire, I then broke down those segments that most affected me. After all, it's all about me, remember?

---

### Business Vision

**Future**

**My role:**

_____

_____

_____

_____

_____

_____

**Things to change about my role:**

_____

_____

_____

_____

_____

*(continued)*

---

**Key people/positions:**

_____

_____

_____

_____

_____

_____

**New growth opportunities:**

_____

_____

_____

_____

_____

**Future accomplishments:**

_____

_____

_____

_____

_____

So I began by projecting *my future role.*

What would I be doing in the organization five years from now? Would I still be the main salesperson or bill payer? (God, I hope not!) As I thought about it, there were a few roles I wanted to subtract (like bill paying), and a few I wanted to add or continue (such as published author, public speaker, and motorcycle ride leader—more on that to come).

How about you? What do *you* want to be doing five years from now? Remember that you don't necessarily need to be in your current company five years from now; I've worked with entrepreneurs whose goal was to transition out of the company in that time period. Whatever you want, be honest with yourself about it, because what you describe here is going to greatly influence the future direction of your organization. It will also affect the composition of your company, which leads to the next question.

I needed to consider *things I would like to change.*

I could have gone one of two ways with this—either playing it safe or really getting creative and going for it. With my personal vision still running through my head, I decided to go all out and began listing drastic transformations to the organization, changes that included reducing my number of local consulting clients from 13 to 4 thereby giving me more time to gain more of a national presence. I also wanted to convert the business into a virtual company that would allow me total mobility. This would help me achieve another one of my goals: spending most of my time on the back of a motorcycle.

I also wanted to retain a minimum of employees and spend more time teaching and speaking to groups of entrepreneurs rather than conducting individual consulting sessions. I figured that I could have a greater impact on entrepreneurs by working collectively with a large group in a room for three days than I could by working with one business at a time. Of course, we would spend the middle part of the day riding through some cool countryside, but that would be icing on the cake for me, as I was really being drawn toward the teaching side of my business.

The thing to remember here is to remain true to your market or, as a longtime client likes to say, "If you make hamburgers, don't start cooking hot dogs." Keep working on your specialty and honing the skills needed to do what what you do well. My future vision for the company needed to mesh with my successful workshop program and capitalize on the experience I'd gained leading and teaching entrepreneurs—or else I'd be off base. But it was still a radical change to my company, so I needed to take a glimpse at the future.

It was time to consider *changes to key people and key positions.*

Whew, here's where the tough change comes in. You now need to look at your company somewhat clinically—not coldly, but in a scientific or quantifiable way. After all, you've just described changes in your role and the company, and this will naturally lead to a change in personnel. When making these changes, you need to look at *positions* or responsibilities first. This way, you avoid the trap of building crucial segments of the company around one person's needs or wants. After all, there's only one person that can afford that luxury, and it's you!

So I began by ascertaining the new job titles I was going to need before I even thought of eliminating some, if any, positions. New titles included meeting planner, scheduler, literary agent, public relations agent, and so on. I then fought the urge to spend a bit of time trying to match up current at-risk positions with the new ones to see if they could be combined. That's a slippery slope that I didn't need to navigate just yet; I'd come back to it later in the process. But it was definitely in the back of my mind, because what made this section so hard was the people involved. My team members all meant a great deal to me, and I was going to do my best to salvage their jobs.

So after that mind-bender, it was time to get a bit more optimistic and consider *new growth opportunities.*

There's nothing more fun for an entrepreneur than envisioning new markets to chase. It's written in our DNA. So I fleshed it out here. I began to outline my ideas for a national Retreat on Wheels, book tour, and national consulting. These were huge undertakings, but hey, these were the types of challenges that any entrepreneur worth his salt lives for—and I was going for it. After all, I was in the prime of my career, I had great health (even with one part missing), and I had a ton of energy.

Think about it, these are the types of challenges you've worked your entire career to prepare for and tackle. It's no time to think small. When you hit this point, be realistic and focused, but *think big!* Because as my first sales manager in business once said to me, "You never want to wake up at age 65, look in the mirror, and say, 'I wish I would have . . .'" Hell no!

Which led to the final thought for the day: *future accomplishments.*

OK, I'd decided where I wanted to go, so what would I do on the way there? I listed my future achievements: my book hits the *New York Times* best sellers list (ballsy, I know), my book tour is sponsored by a major motorcycle manufacturer, I speak before hundreds of people about my Navigation Process, and I ride with some of the coolest CEOs and entrepreneurs on the planet. I went on a bit longer, but you get the idea.

This isn't the time for self-doubt, and if you're like me, you have to fight through the feeling that it's all just a pipe dream. And that's where it got damned easy to doubt myself, especially after all I'd been through. After all, who was I to dream this big? But then a wonderful quote to which I've subscribed my entire adult life slowly rolled through my brain, the standard from Napoleon Hill: "Whatever a mind can conceive and believe, it can achieve."

That principle is the essence of being an entrepreneur. If I allowed any uncertainty to rule my thoughts, then I'd just as soon pull up a chair and turn on Dr. Phil, since I would have gone into "oh, woe is me" mode instead of grabbing my business by the handlebars like I needed to. That descent into self-pity avoided, I turned off the conscious portion of my brain and got lost in the rest of the ride. We rolled through the lovely Fraser River Valley, with its tall peaks and hillsides covered with dark pines and aspens. Our final destination on this leg was Winter Park, but before we got there, we detoured through Rocky Mountain National Park, where we were forced to change from short-sleeved shirts and jeans to full leather gear in a matter of minutes. Gotta love the mountains!

After that superb experience, we pulled up to the Gasthaus Eichler. It's one of the coolest mom-and-pop hotels you'll ever find, mainly because the owner is the former head chef of the renowned Beaver Creek Lodge and serves up food that's to die for. That night I drank killer wine while feasting on homemade German sausages of all shapes and sizes. Remember that I'm Cajun and have eaten some incredible meals in my day, so take it to the bank when I tell you that this was one of the best on record.

One thing for sure is that I got no further work done that night, thanks to the many glasses of wine and port I enjoyed with my cigar out on the back patio. The work was to be tackled the next morning when, once again, I was up at sunrise with nobody around. Winter Park isn't that large a town, so I walked a couple of blocks in either direction and finally found an early bird café where I bought a large cup of hot coffee. I then returned to the patio, started to sort out my thoughts, and worked on getting them into a coherent and workable outline.

On a clean sheet of my notepad, I titled the page Personal Outline and created three columns: Key Result Areas (KRA) on the left, Present in the middle, and Future on the right. Under the KRA column, I listed my major categories: Family, Health, Learning, Financial, Spirituality, and Community. From there, I simply went down my list from the prior brainstorming session and placed the items in the corresponding columns. For example, "favorite ways to spend my time" went under Present, while "things I want to do" went under Future, and so on.

| **Personal Outline** | | |
|---|---|---|
| Key Result Areas | Present | Future |
| Family | • _____ <br> • _____ <br> • _____ <br> • _____ | • _____ <br> • _____ <br> • _____ <br> • _____ |
| Health | • _____ <br> • _____ <br> • _____ <br> • _____ | • _____ <br> • _____ <br> • _____ <br> • _____ |
| Spiritual | • _____ <br> • _____ <br> • _____ <br> • _____ | • _____ <br> • _____ <br> • _____ <br> • _____ |
| Financial | • _____ <br> • _____ <br> • _____ <br> • _____ | • _____ <br> • _____ <br> • _____ <br> • _____ |
| Recreation | • _____ <br> • _____ <br> • _____ <br> • _____ | • _____ <br> • _____ <br> • _____ <br> • _____ |
| Community | • _____ <br> • _____ <br> • _____ <br> • _____ | • _____ <br> • _____ <br> • _____ <br> • _____ |
| Learning | • _____ <br> • _____ <br> • _____ | • _____ <br> • _____ <br> • _____ |

I then moved on to my Business Outline. However, my major categories were different here. Along with Financial and Learning, I also included categories such as Sales, Marketing, and Community Involvement, as well as a Miscellaneous category for those items that didn't clearly fit into any of the others. Then, as before, I simply placed the items listed in either the corresponding Present or Future column.

| Business Outline | | |
|---|---|---|
| Key Result Areas | Present | Future |
| Growth (Company/Personnel) | • _____ <br> • _____ <br> • _____ <br> • _____ | • _____ <br> • _____ <br> • _____ <br> • _____ |
| Personnel | • _____ <br> • _____ <br> • _____ <br> • _____ | • _____ <br> • _____ <br> • _____ <br> • _____ |
| Financial | • _____ <br> • _____ <br> • _____ <br> • _____ | • _____ <br> • _____ <br> • _____ <br> • _____ |
| Sales | • _____ <br> • _____ <br> • _____ <br> • _____ | • _____ <br> • _____ <br> • _____ <br> • _____ |

| Key Result Areas | Present | Future |
|---|---|---|
| Marketing | • _____ <br> • _____ <br> • _____ <br> • _____ | • _____ <br> • _____ <br> • _____ <br> • _____ |
| Learning | • _____ <br> • _____ <br> • _____ <br> • _____ | • _____ <br> • _____ <br> • _____ <br> • _____ |
| Miscellaneous | • _____ <br> • _____ <br> • _____ <br> • _____ | • _____ <br> • _____ <br> • _____ <br> • _____ |

The purpose of this outline was to organize my thoughts and give me a quick one-page reference as I turned my attention back to what began this entire process—answering *The Question.*

*It's five years from now and my entire life has gone according to plan—every challenge overcome, every goal achieved. What does it look like?*

Well, here is the Answer I wrote:

*It's five years from today, and I'm cruising through the mountains on the back of a motorcycle. The past half decade has been a wonderful and challenging transition from Navigator to author/lecturer/workshop leader. My book was published two and a half years ago to great acclaim, which led to public speaking and engagements and the successful launch of my Entrepreneur's Retreat on Wheels.*

*I have trimmed my local client base down to four, while attracting numerous other clients from around the country. This allows me to touch people while spending more time on the road exploring everything that this beautiful country has to offer. And that is exactly what I'm doing this week as I lead a group of top CEOs on a three-day ride in order to work on their businesses. Yes, life and business are truly good.*

Remember, don't go into a great deal of detail here. It doesn't have to be a lengthy reply, just a clean, concise summary of what your life will look like once you incorporate all the changes you've included in your various responses to the questions above. The outline you create from these answers is designed to give you a clear picture of where you are today (Present column) while identifying those new elements that make up your tomorrow (Future column). The Answer simply requires you to create a snapshot of what your future looks like.

But, you ask, what about focusing on the small stuff? Where is the detail you talked about before? Hang on, we'll get there in the next couple of chapters. But before we do, a quick story on figuring out the difference between Potential and Success:

## *The Question* Case Study: Potential versus Success

Ten years before I began this journey of life examination, I began to work with two brothers who had inherited an already-successful company from their father. Since taking over the firm, Mark the CEO, and Dave, the senior vice president, have continued its profitable run by doubling annual revenues while maintaining its position as industry leader in the state. Just two years apart in age and now in their mid-forties, both are looking at life beyond the company and asked my assistance in answering the question "What's next?"

The organization is currently divided into two distinct divisions, each with tremendous upside *potential*. The first delivers the company's primary service, and the second operates as fabrication support to the first. Each division is run by a strong vice president of operations with a track record of profitability. As Mark and Dave look to the future, their only real concern is with the fabrication support division. Originally set up to service the main line of business, this branch has grown beyond the company's needs and sells its excess output to many of the firm's competitors.

Over time, the fabrication support vice president had convinced the brothers to branch out and build two new plants in two neighboring states that showed *potential*. His theory was that the plants would grow quickly; they would not be viewed as threats by the competition, since the company's primary business did not service those markets. This issue of competition was, in the vice president's mind, hindering further growth within their home state, which is why he had wanted to venture elsewhere.

Now, like any start-up ventures, both of the new locations—despite showing much promise—were also money pits. The losses incurred at these facilities were blamed on inefficient work flow, a factor that made them less than competitive in the marketplace. The vice president was therefore pitching the notion that new, more modern plants were the answer. After much deliberation, Mark and Dave gave the go-ahead to build a new, modern plant in one of the

(*continued*)

locations, and within a few months the wheels began to fall off for the two of them emotionally.

On one hand, the new locations were in prime areas poised for growth. On the other, each was separated geographically and philosophically from the core company. This posed a management challenge in terms of the plants' day to day oversight, and therein lay Mark and Dave's struggle with the demons of *potential* versus their true vision of *success*. The brothers' entrepreneurial business instincts said that over time, these investments would pay off and perhaps also lead to the expansion of their core business into those new markets, but it still didn't feel right to them.

The internal turmoil that Mark and Dave were feeling also caused a new problem within the organization—indecision. With so much on the line now, they were no longer as confident as they had been before. And that brought to the surface two fundamental questions that needed answering: Why were they investing in this new direction and these new locations? Was the growth *really* necessary to the company? Both were good questions, but in the end, the issue hinged on the real question: Was this what they really *wanted* to do?

What didn't feel right about this decision was the impact it would have on the future of their lives. Investing in new markets is a risky, long-term play. It requires intense focus and energy in order to pull it off successfully, and neither Mark nor Dave was certain that he could make that kind of commitment. Therefore, our meetings weren't just focused on business. We also discussed the very question that I answered myself in the previous chapter: What do you want your life to look like in the next five years and beyond? To help find the answers, we used *The Question* and The

Questionnaire, and combined with their business research, this turned into an in-depth process that lasted months. During this time, one brother literally went into the mountains for a while, and the other took off on his sailboat to think things through.

We all met one fateful Friday and included their father in the discussion. The meeting turned into an eight-hour roller-coaster of emotions. The three family members openly and clearly stated where they wanted the company to go, from the standpoint of how it was to fit within their lives. In an incredible display of group candor they stopped, dug deep, and asked, "Why? What made us decide to support this expansion, and why did we feel that it was a necessary step for the company?" They recognized that while it had been a good *business* decision, at the end of the day, it was a poor *life* decision. Neither brother wanted to expend the energy or take the risk necessary to support the new plants' growth.

The final decision was not only to shut down the two new locations, but to downsize the fabrication division and refocus it on the company's own internal needs rather than creating excess output to sell to its competitors. The short-term cost was a significant loss of investment dollars and the immediate release of the division's vice president. Not an easy decision to make and one that, for a while, sent shock waves throughout the organization. However, within two short years, the renewed focus resulted in 30 percent growth and the doubling of the most important number: net profit.

Today, Dave and Mark are happier, wealthier, and much better off for having had the courage to chase their own vision of success, rather than attempting to respond to the demands of business potential. The company has a clear

*(continued)*

vision, and succession plans for both brothers are in place and moving forward, all because they stopped and took the time to determine their Ultimate Destination in life and focused their economic engine on that. They identified the type of ride they wanted and the associated finish lines that would fuel their competitive juices—while also feeding their souls.

 ## Road Rules

- Find your getaway place and take the all the time you need to think through the outline.
- Identify and reconcile the gap between your company's potential and your personal version of success.
- You must account for the past and present before you can get a true picture of the future.

*You can access my free tools to help you Figure It Out, along with detailed instructions, on my web site at www.BikersGuidetoBusiness.com.*

CHAPTER 11

# Your Economic Engine

*At some point, you have to plant a flag on the map.*

On the last real riding day of my Colorado bike tour and before leaving my hotel, the Gasthaus Eichler, I enjoyed one last culinary treat from René, the owner and chef, who whipped up an incredible breakfast of homemade sausages and the lightest pancakes I've ever eaten. Normally he wouldn't have been in the kitchen at that early hour, but René's a biker and a friend of my guide, Tom's, so he made it a point to personally prepare breakfast for us. After swapping a few riding stories, René left Tom and me to discuss the day's ride and our ultimate destination: Mount Evans, which has the highest paved road in North America.

This was our last ride of the week, and the journey out of Winter Park was nothing short of breathtaking. As we rolled south on Highway 40, topping 11,000 feet over Berthoud Pass, all I could think was, "Man, oh man, what a way to start the day!" From that point, we headed down into the town of Empire and on to Idaho Springs. Going up Highway 103, we climbed back to 10,000 feet and stopped at the Echo Lake Lodge before riding to the summit.

While resting and sipping a cup of hot chocolate, I did what every biker does when in a new place: I wandered through the neat old historic building looking for a T-shirt to buy. Now, if there's one piece of advice I'd give to the lodge, it would be to hire a new T-shirt designer. This is because, like most bikers, I am a connoisseur of such T-shirts. I own a huge stack of them (all black), and together they tell the story of the many places I've been. It's a very personalized collection that I wear with pride to bike fests and biker bars, so finding the right T-shirt on any ride is sort of important to me.

This time, however, my search was proving to be somewhat of a struggle, since none of the shirts particularly spoke to me. I finally settled on one that exclaimed that "I made it up Mt. Evans!" How lame is that? I knew that I'd probably never wear the damned thing, but at least I would have it to remind me of my upcoming accomplishment. Now all I had to do was actually *ride* to the top and back without falling off the mountain, which I feared was a very real possibility.

But then again, I'd probably be OK, because the cool thing about this weeklong tour was the way that Tom navigated it. When leaving Conifer our first day, we mostly rode through flatlands, and each passing day took us systematically through higher and higher ground. This is important for a flatlander rider like me, because it helped me to gradually adjust to the higher terrain and ward off the altitude sickness that can afflict some people. After all, the last thing you need when on two wheels is to lose your faculties, especially when riding up a mountain with no guardrail.

Tom's method of touring also served to hone my mountain riding skills, which needed to be at their best because the road up to the summit is not your regular highway and was definitely the ultimate riding challenge for the trip. The switch-backs (U-shaped curves in the road) are so tight that at times I was looking at myself going and coming at the same time! And did I mention that there's no guardrail? Let's just say that I'm happy the week prepared me well for both the altitude and the steering challenges.

The road to the summit is 14 grueling miles long and even-tually tops out at 14,262 feet. The ride to the top and back takes approximately two hours. And as if the prospect of taking that long to go 28 miles wasn't enough to make me pause, before setting out we stopped at the guard's gate to ask how the weather was on the peak. The guard informed us that there was the pos-sibility of drastic weather changes between here and the top, but that this was just a typical day on the mountain. And yes, there was definitely a storm coming, but people weren't being ordered off the mountain *yet*. Nice. When starting our ascent, the only thing that kept the prospect of a storm rolling in off my mind was Tom's suggestion that I catch the look of terror on the faces of the cagers (people in cars) as they drive by. I must admit that it was amusing, and I actually laughed out loud more than once.

The ride up was fascinating in other ways as well. Along with the intensity of knowing I couldn't afford to make a mistake, I experienced the most surreal view when rolling through some of the more extreme switchbacks. When bikers are taking a corner, they're taught to look at where they're going and trust that the bike will follow. This made for an eerie way of catching incredible scenery while literally looking backwards. When not navigating switchbacks, I saw trees that proved that only the gnarly can survive at this altitude, and interesting little round holes in the center of the roadway where varmints poked their heads through every now and then. Man, as if the ride wasn't challenging enough, in addition to watching out for the terrified cagers, I was now concerned that some weird member of the mole family was going to reach out and lock me up while I was navigating some of the most intense switchbacks known to man. I was totally up on the handlebars!

But all of the physical and mental work that you're required to do on the ride up is well worth the effort, and the mere notion of hardship vanishes the moment that you get to the top. It was cold, to be sure, at least 30 degrees colder than at the base. But the view was *spectacular*. I was once again looking over the tops of clouds and caught a glimpse of Denver beyond the incredible range of mountains before me. I then looked down the side of the mountain and watched mountain goats and a couple of bighorn sheep climb up and down. It was definitely one of those *wow* moments in life.

After only 30 minutes at the peak, we made our way back down and stopped at the 12,000-foot level to take pictures of the snowfields at Summit Lake. We then continued down to the lodge and stopped long enough to remove some of the layers of clothing that had been needed to keep us from freezing when we were up at the top. Then it was time to reverse course and head back down to Echo Lake, east on 103, and down through Squaw Pass to the eventual end of the ride.

I tell the story of my ride up Mount Evans not only to share the exhilaration of riding to such an altitude, but also to keep with the business/biker metaphor. No, I'll not be so lame as to use that ride as the old "lessons learned from the top of the mountain" image; instead, I'll use the entire week's ride as a metaphor for the Navigation Process. Looking back on Tom's method of touring, I realized that the one and only thing he knew about me when starting out on our ride together was that I was an experienced rider. But *experienced* can mean different things to different people, and the only other thing he knew for sure was that I wanted to ride the mountains and eventually tackle the highest road there is.

So like any prudent tour guide, Tom broke the trip down into the appropriate legs, each of which tested my skills and abilities along the way. Every day's ride built on and continued fittingly from the one before, and he eventually felt confident that I could safely navigate my way to the summit of Mount Evans. Tom knew that if he tried to take me from our starting point in Conifer all the way through to Mount Evans on the very first day, I'd have been more than a little intimidated and barely retained anything he said. So instead he broke the week down into the appropriate number of rides at the appropriate level of difficulty, and briefed me each morning on where we were going that day and what to expect. Of course, there were always variables and challenges to be met along the way, but at least I had an idea of the lay of the land and had been given the opportunity to say yes or no to the route before turning my face into the wind and riding.

And that brings us to the focus of this chapter. After doing the heavy lifting associated with deep reflection and discovering where I wanted to go in life, it was time to figure out how to rally my fellow riders—my team—around a vision. In order to do that, I needed to use Tom's technique to break down the five-year vision that I had developed into *legs of the trip,* because if I couldn't get my team behind me I was toast.

In biking, I can simply point to a spot on the map and describe the route and destination to everyone, but in business it's not that simple. I had to overcome the fact that my mission's central theme was now my personal agenda, and there's no way to rally a team solely around what *I* want out of life. After all, why should my colleagues care about the goals toward which I'm personally driving five years into the future? They, too, come to work every day in order to achieve their own hopes and dreams, not just to help me realize my own. Therefore, I needed to bring the objective down to a common denominator, one that my entire team could embrace and support.

I had to recognize my company for what it really was—an economic engine built specifically to take me and my team where we wanted to go in life. This was a foreign concept to me, though, because as an entrepreneur I was geared to put the *company* first and simply let my daily life revolve around it. I tended to "live what I do" 24/7 and harbored a false sense of indispensability, which was really just a fear that the place would fall apart in my absence. I wasn't alone in this, either; it was also a common issue among my clients. But I realized that it was time to break through it.

On the surface, that simple change in perspective took it away from being all about me to again being all about the company. And yes, I clearly stated earlier that it was no longer healthy to focus solely on company goals to the detriment of my personal goals. However, in this instance, it was OK because I knew the company direction and focus would match that of my personal life. And that put me back into my sweet spot as an entrepreneur and removed me from the role I had grown used to, in which the company overshadowed—or eliminated altogether—my personal goals.

I then referred back to The Questionnaire and pulled out the business information needed to paint a clear picture, vision, and mission for myself and for my team of where my company needed to go. I needed to create a *Scenario* from which we could collectively create a plan.

Scenario Planning entered the world of business in the early 1970s. Royal Dutch/Shell implemented and utilized this technique as a process for generating and evaluating its strategic options during the oil embargo. It was originally used by analysts to create simulation games for policy makers. As a result of that company's success, many of the larger organizations throughout the world started to use this technique. It is now standard operating procedure when companies are trying to look to the future.

Scenario Planning starts with a fundamental axiom: *You can't get there from here, but you can always get here from there.* Essentially, this means that you have to start with the end in mind. I first heard this phrase in the early 1990s, when the moderator for our local public school system used it to open a three-day strategic planning and design shop. When he first said it, most of us in the room blankly stared at him, until someone asked the question that seemed to be on everyone's mind: "What's the difference?" He told us to think about a goal we have 12 to 24 months down the road and ask ourselves: What's the first thing you see? We gave a variety of different responses, all of which were associated with things that we needed to overcome in order to get there. He then asked that we turn our vision around and think of that same goal as having been accomplished and behind us. *Now* what did we see? By looking at the situation this way, we no longer saw obstacles or tasks that had to be done. Instead, we saw these as tasks that had already been accomplished.

The power behind that minor shift in perception is that it allows creativity and ideas to flow much more easily. You've eliminated the limitations associated with having to do some-thing and can instead consider these to-dos to be done. There are no more obstacles, which leaves you free to identify and focus on even the smallest details needed to accomplish the goal. And that makes a ton of difference, because like most people, I—along with my team—tend to get bogged down with these obstacles.

Another factor to keep in mind when building a Scenario is the need to determine the right time and distance. Major corporations routinely create Scenarios 5 or 10 years out into the future, but in an entrepreneurial organization that length of time won't work. Things fly at us too fast and we have to react accordingly. Therefore, my experience has shown that it's easier for me and my team to wrap our heads around a Scenario that's limited to one year in the future. Anything longer than this causes us to lose our sense of urgency and focus, making it nearly impossible to cross finish lines on time.

Also, when composing the Scenario, it's important to give only bottom-line details in your description of the company's position 12 months down the line. I always list major goals: gross revenue, types of services and products that we've sold, the status of the team (additions, subtractions), product development, and the like. I may throw in a few new twists from year to year, such as a new management position or a promotion for a key team member, but the basic, underlying outline remains the same. I then weave these goals into a paragraph or two that paints a clear picture of what the organization will look like. I always write it as if I'm reporting to someone like my banker or presenting a state of the company message to my team.

In order to help with the process of synthesizing the information from my Questionnaire, I created a worksheet that helps me identify the *Key Result Areas* (KRAs) and critical factors upon which we need to focus in the upcoming year. The tough things to do are to stay at the 5,000-foot level with the information, and to avoid including any detailed how-tos in the write-up that might limit my colleagues' thinking. I simply want to describe the end result in a way that allows the team to come up with the how-to answers, and ensure that the team buys into the company's path for success.

The first items I listed were the Key Result Areas critical to our success in the coming year. (You might also list items such as new locations, new positions, financial goals, product sales, and so on.)

- Maintain and grow current client base
- Finish book
- Develop web site
- Increase public speaking

- Market the Navigation workshop
- Begin the business/biker poster line

I then listed the *Boundaries or Limiting Factors* to our growth. (Other items that may apply are new and old competitors, staffing changes, economic conditions, and so on.)

- 10 percent increase in revenue
- Stable team
- Cramped office space
- Lack of knowledge in the book publishing area
- Limited funds to launch poster line

I then took into account any additional factors not covered in the first two categories, such as training needs, new information, or perceived market changes.

- Research and attend conferences on publishing
- Research and find strategic partners for poster line (designer and printer)
- Propose partnership with major motorcycle manufacturer

I then used this information to formulate the following Scenario:

*It's December 31, 20___ and my five-year plan continues to be on track. The three conferences and workshops I attended this past year helped me develop my book, which was purchased by a major publisher and will hit the shelves next year. The book contract opened doors with two major motorcycle manufacturers, and we are currently discussing partnership opportunities in the areas of speaking and workshops.*

*On the corporate side, we expanded our current client base by 10 percent—with no additional team members or office space—which helped to offset the cost of launching the line of business/biker posters. The increase in revenue along with the two new partners in the venture helped to complete the poster design and launch the web site by the end of the third quarter.*

*How did we do this?*

**Note:** My Scenario was at the 10,000 ft. level and spoke to the major goals I wanted to accomplish in the coming year: a contract with a book publisher, conferences, partnership talks, business/biker posters, a web site, and client revenue. This was my symbolic planting of the flag on a map for my team, so that they could clearly see where we wanted and needed to go. The detail necessary to get there would come in the next phase of the process, during the Tactical Planning Session (which I'll describe in the next chapter).

My business is unique, so obviously my Scenario will not work for you and your business. Here is a template version that may better suit your needs as you move forward:

*It's December 31, 20___ and our company has achieved the goal of $___ in revenue. A major contributor to this success was our expanding into two new market locations: the first in (location 1), and the second in (location 2). We opened these markets with a limited increase in overall debt and a 10 percent increase in staff. These openings also allowed us to continue promoting from within, and we have therefore grown the senior leadership team by two members.*

*The hiring and retention program we instituted has had a great impact, resulting in our overall employee turnover ending the year below 4 percent. The retention of key employees has had a positive effect on net income, which has increased by ____ percent or $____.*

*How did we do this?*

Once you've written your Scenario, apply the following set of questions to it to ensure it's composed properly and will give you the desired result in the next phase of the process.

### Scenario Questions
- Is the Scenario compatible with your long-term objectives?
- Is it focused?
- Does it give you a clear picture of the mission?
- Does the Scenario push the company's growing edge?
- Does it include specific, measurable objectives?
- Are the goals realistically achievable in the time frame?
- Are the issues easily identified?

Your Scenario is the foundation for your next stage in the Navigation Process. It's very important that once you compose your Scenario, you do *not* share it with team members prior to the Tactical Planning Session outlined in the next chapter. Your team will be best served if it answers the Scenario questions immediately and from the gut. You—and they—will have plenty of time after the next phase to do research. However, you only have one chance to elicit their instinctive answers.

Now that you've composed a workable Scenario, it's time to build your plan.

## Road Rules

- Keep your Scenario business focused—do not include personal goals.
- Stay specific but avoid going into too much detail when composing your Scenario.
- Plan no more than 18 months in advance.
- The Scenario must paint a clear picture of where you are going.

---

*You can access my free tools to help you build a killer Scenario, along with detailed instructions, on my web site at www.BikersGuidetoBusiness.com.*

 CHAPTER 12

# Planning Your Ride

After a week on the road, I was somewhat sad to return the rental bike to the dealership. I walked away hoping that it wouldn't take too long for me to come back to these high roads. The experience of riding across and through the Rockies exceeded all of my expectations, and the mental journey was an added bonus as I moved forward. The week was a success, as far as I was concerned. It got me far enough away from the day-to-day grind of the business to clear my head, and I felt really good about the new direction in which I was heading.

The great thing about riding the open road is that it allows me to stop the noise in my head, thereby opening my mind up to new possibilities in my world. On this particular ride, I was able to reflect on the life and business decisions that had brought me to this current space. From there, I was able to project my future direction with clarity and confidence, all of which made it easier for me to develop a realistic Scenario of where my company needed to be in one year's time. I was now ready for the next phase of the process: I needed to build a plan.

*Plan* is one of those four-letter words most entrepreneurs hate to hear, and the act of planning is something we hate to engage in. It's also one of the reasons I left corporate America in the first place. The mere memory of the tortuous planning process causes me to roll my eyes, groan out loud, and want to blow it off all together.

If you're a corporate refugee like me, you know what I'm talking about. Those traditional three-day strategic planning sessions are a painful reminder of bad times—and something to be avoided at all costs. I gave up countless days of my life working on some upper-level-management schmuck's plan that did nothing more than hit the shelf after 60 days, never to be seen again.

Almost as though I was one of Pavlov's dogs, this traditional method of planning conditioned me to believe that any plan put down on paper had to be massive. And who, in today's fast-paced business world, has time to read, much less *write,* something that long? The corporations I've worked for all operated under the notion that more meant better, because they mistakenly believed that lengthy strategic planning sessions produce detailed plans. They actually thought that a longer planning time ensured we'd uncover everything that we needed to build a successful strategy.

But they were wrong, because spending that much time together caused us to be sloppy. Lengthy meetings allowed for too many presentations and discussions, thereby killing any sense of urgency in the room. And all anyone *really* wanted after the first day of boring graphs and presentations was to get the hell out of that room. These endless soapbox negotiations caused our minds to wander, and we ultimately skipped over a ton of key details and tasks that at the time seemed insignificant. This extreme level of boredom guaranteed that whatever plan we came up with would be more BS than substance.

Then, like some time-released virus, these seemingly insignificant details began to grow and eventually gummed up the organization's performance. Months down the road, we found ourselves reacting time and again to missed targets and deadlines, which led to a knee-jerk change in strategy merely to regain control. Each time we changed strategy, our employees had to react, and each time they were called upon to react, they rolled their eyes and moved ever more slowly. After all, they wondered, why should they rush? Things would only change again in a month or so. To this day, I break into a cold sweat when walking into a hotel ballroom from the memory of such futility.

But futility aside, as the leader of a small business, I simply cannot afford to spend three days talking *about* the business. I came to this realization by being nimble and relying mainly on my passion and wits. The downside to this is that I find myself adopting a somewhat simplistic mind-set—when something positive hits, I'll automatically follow that direction. If something is negative or destructive, I'll close my mind to it and go the other way. Who needs a plan to do *that?*

The need to plan goes beyond that tired old cliché, "If you fail to plan, you plan to fail." That's pretty much bull, as I've met many entrepreneurs who've never planned a day in their lives and have still managed to build solid organizations. However, the downside for them of never planning is that they are still running their organizations as hard today as when they began, with no real break in sight. And while that level of passion and commitment is OK, the energy that is required of them day after day will eventually wear down even the best entrepreneur. I know, because this is where I found myself. That is when I realized that it was time to assume a different approach.

Now, I consider myself a pretty good planner, but like most entrepreneurs, I am more likely to do my planning on the fly. I think that's because our organizations are usually small and we feel like we know everything that goes on within the company on a daily basis. We feel that since we have all of the necessary information in our heads, we can design our plans in a vacuum and roll them out to everyone on an as-needed basis. After all, it's our company, and the employees who can't follow our lead just don't "think like we do" or "can't see the big picture." To be sure, our employees' input may or may not change the plan dramatically. This style of planning usually creates a situation where we're constantly up on the handlebars of the company, micromanaging it and everyone in it on a daily basis. And that will eventually frustrate even the most patient soul out there.

I've learned that I need to manage less when every one of my key team members is involved in the planning session. I do not look to them for direction, as that should never be provided by a committee, and should be established through the Scenario process described in the previous chapter. Instead, I use the planning process to establish focus, gain their buy-in, and get their help in developing the key tactics. I want to ensure that they all know what *I know* they need to do.

Since leaving the corporate world, I've discovered that planning doesn't have to be painful. I've realized that attending so many poorly run planning sessions actually helped me to create a process that really works. I did it with the simple premise that *planning is nothing more than stopping to think about the things you know you need to do before you do them, and writing it all down on paper*.

Simply put, it's about identifying the *work to be done*. The plan is a road map, not a novel. Along with being simple and easy to read, a good plan will prevent key tasks from falling through the cracks and will keep an organization focused on its goals. It is also important for the plan to harness the "do what it takes" attitude prevalent in all entrepreneurial companies. This approach is absolutely crucial to a company's daily survival and progress; if the plan doesn't serve this function—even for just one team member—it will eventually stunt an organization's growth.

We've all experienced some degree of team dissention or division. In biking, it's the fellow rider who leaves the pack to go off and explore for a while. It may be well intentioned at the time, but it leaves the road captain wondering where the hell he went off to. The pack eventually catches up to him sitting on the side of the road waiting on everyone, and he eventually folds back into the pack. But what if you needed his riding expertise closer to the front? And what does this say to the rest of the pack—that it's OK to do your own thing as long as you have good intentions?

In business a situation likes this arises when all the members of an organization apply their individual agendas to a group goal. They all run around doing whatever task crosses their paths, whenever it comes along. Sure, they can do it, but *should* they do it? How do all team members know whether this task is really being completed when it's supposed to be—or if it's simply being done now because this is when it's most convenient?

One task may seem like a little thing; after all, it all needs to be done. But this lack of coordination will eventually cause unnecessary bottlenecks in your daily work flow that show up in the form of overtime, as employees work frantically to meet soon-to-be-missed deadlines. These daily self-imposed firefights serve to ramp up the pressure and stress level within the organization, and eventually lead to burnout. A good plan doesn't just consist of a list of tasks waiting to be randomly checked off. It should also identify the method and timing for handling each task, thereby ensuring that team members do them in the right order and at the right time.

Another key factor that I took into account when designing the planning process is that as an entrepreneur I don't have the luxury of spending days or weeks planning. I can't afford to distract the entire team for long periods of time, nor do I need to end up with some big honking binder that eventually sits on a shelf, totally forgotten after 60 days or so. And—though my consulting brethren will kill me for saying so—entrepreneurs cannot always afford to hire some expensive consultant to facilitate the planning process, either.

Keeping all of that in mind, I wanted a process that would fit into the fast-paced and hectic world of an entrepreneur. It needed to quickly tap the team's collective experience in a matter of a few highly focused hours and produce a straightforward road map that would be easy to use. Instead of that big binder, I wanted an Action Item List no more than two pages in length that effectively identified the tactics upon which each team member needs to focus daily, weekly, and monthly in order to turn the business Scenario into reality and take us where we need to go. Kind of like a GPS map that gives me the flexibility to easily zoom out or zoom in as needed.

So over the course of many years of working with clients and with my own company, I designed the following Tactical Planning Process. Here's how it works.

## Preparation

Much like the plan you end up with, a successful Tactical Planning Session needs to be simple and to the point. It requires only a few items:

1. **The right team members in the room.** This group can include individuals outside of your immediate management team. My rule of thumb is to identify all who directly touch the plan and will be responsible for implementing any of the Key Result Areas. If they have a part in it, they need to be present.

2. **No prework or research.** I've found that if you assign prework or research, you end up with a more politically correct or rehearsed response to the process instead of the answers that you really want. I want my employees' immediate gut reaction to the questions I'm asking; having them think too much prior to the planning keeps me from getting their candid thoughts on the organization today and in the future.

3. **The completed Scenario.** I absolutely, positively *do not* share the Scenario with anyone prior to the meeting. It goes along with my rule prohibiting prework or research; again, this is because I do not want to hear the politically correct response. I want to hear what my team members *really* think.

4. **A meeting area with plenty of empty wall space and room for team members to spread out and work.** I highly recommend that you hold the Tactical Planning Session off-site in order to limit distractions. It's easier than you might think to find low-cost facilities. The main thing to remember is that the space you select should have ample room to spread out. Do not use the traditional boardroom table; each person needs room to think and work individually. Also, there's never really a need for a video presentation, so you don't need to worry about video equipment. However, wall space is very important, as you want sufficient room to hold the Post-it-style flip chart sheets the group members will use to answer the questions. You will need to group their answers on the wall throughout the planning session.

5. **Tools.** You'll need one or two pads of large Post-it-style flip chart paper, along with a large marker for every participant.

6. **A facilitator.** As I said a bit earlier, there's no need for some expensive consultant to lead this process. However, I find that it's more productive to have an outsider navigating the session, because this will allow the usual team leader to act as a true participant. It's not completely necessary, however, to have an outside facilitator; the process of asking and responding to the questions is designed to allow me, or any other leader, to both facilitate and participate.

7. **Someone to take notes.** I always have someone who is not a participant attend and record the individual

responses for me on a laptop in real time. This way, I literally walk out of the room with my plan already documented.

## Getting Started

I take the first 30 minutes or so to open the session with a short recap of how the organization got to where it is today and share my 10,000-foot-level overview of its potential. This offers everyone in the room a baseline perspective of the company and is also a great time to be very positive about our accomplishments. I also joke about our challenges and failures, making sure to relay the lessons learned and point out how those experiences have made us a better organization going forward.

One very important thing I always do is stop the discussion when covering the present day and how the company is positioned for the future. This is *not* the time to go into the Scenario, as doing so will hinder your planning. Be patient—you'll get there in short order.

Before beginning the working session, I cover the necessary housekeeping items, such as restroom locations and the schedule for breaks and lunch. After that, I break for five minutes to give everyone a chance to take a restroom break and replenish their coffee before launching into the questions.

## Asking the Questions

Having sat through literally hundreds of planning sessions in my career, I've learned that good questioning will always make or break any gathering. The way in which you ask and answer the questions (rhythm, order, and pace) is crucial to developing a successful plan *quickly*. Therefore, do not skip or change the order of the questions leading up to the Scenario. The Tactical Planning questions are designed to build on each other and capture the individual thoughts of all team members in the room—all the while, building toward the plan.

On the surface, the first three questions may appear to be rather fundamental; however, they are designed to create the right mind-set for the participants. I've come to understand that all participants come into the meeting with their own set of daily pressures, distractions, and agendas that, if not properly dealt with, can hinder their effectiveness. So I borrowed a page from the retail world. Just as the first 30 feet of a well-designed department store are intended to get you in the mood to shop, the first three questions are designed to get everyone on the same mental page. These questions serve to clear the participants' minds of most side agendas by having them list and actively discuss their priorities and needs for the day, followed by the strengths of the company and opportunities within the marketplace.

I also inject the element of time into my queries in order to foster a sense of urgency. As stated earlier, I'm most interested in gut responses, and I've found that the added pressure of time pushes an experienced team to answer more instinctively, getting us to the point more quickly.

## Answering the Questions

Too often, planning sessions are dominated by one or more people who ramble on about their ideas and leave little time for group discussion. The other participants must either be ballsy enough to take the floor from them in order to get their own points across, or stay quiet.

When two people jockey for position, they inadvertently take everyone down their thought path and stunt the group's overall creativity. On the flip side, every team has individuals who, for various reasons, do not feel comfortable in voicing their opinions in a large group. These are the team members who are turned off by having to fight to have their voices heard. Either case creates a less-than-effective environment in which valuable information is lost. And in any organization, regardless of its size, you simply cannot afford to lose the brain power of even a single person. If you do, the plan will surely suffer.

Therefore, it's important to prevent grandstanding while still allowing for constructive group dialogue. The best way I've found to avoid having anyone dominate the discussion is to have each team member respond individually. This way, you can collect everyone's thoughts and information out in the open before the discussion begins.

This is where the large Post-it-style flip chart paper comes into play; each person in the room should receive a sheet of this paper, along with a large marker. I have all participants put their names at the top and write large so everyone can read their responses from across the room.

The order in which the responses are given is important. I have found that the best way to have the team reply to the questions is by beginning with the person who is newest with the company—or lowest on the totem pole—and proceed up the chain of command (based on seniority and position), with the boss answering last. My experience is that if you or your senior people speak first, others will be less inclined to openly share their opinions and much of their perspective will be lost.

So, keeping that order in mind, when the time allotted to answer the question is up, I have each person post their response on the wall and read it to the group. I don't allow any interruptions or questions until that person has presented his or her entire list. I then open the discussion for a minute or two of *clarification questions* only, in other words, questions that will glean greater understanding of the concept, not lead to a formal debate of ideas. Some examples are "Tell me more about your idea in handling . . ." And "What do you mean by . . .?"

I work hard to avoid those "Have you thought about . . . ?" questions, at least at this stage of the game. As facilitator, I want to guard against questions leading to an open discussion in which challenges and new ideas are thrown out before each person has their say. I simply ask the participants to hold that thought or question, as all will be discussed later in the process. This simple tactic easily prevents anyone from dominating the room and ensures that the shy or new person's voice is heard. I also group the responses on the wall by question instead of by the individual responder. This makes it easier to take notes on particular topics, and it helps the team refer back to each question when needed later in the process.

Now that we've covered the process, here are the questions and some advice on how to administer them.

## Question 1: What result do you want to see at the end of the planning session? (10 minutes)

I always begin with this question because while all the team members know that they're here to participate in a planning session, they all have different opinions of what they would like to discuss and how the day should go. This question gives everyone a chance to voice those views. It's important that both you and your team members see the overarching theme the group is looking to tackle. The typical answers range from company goals to growth strategies, marketing strategies, support needed, and more—the possibilities are endless.

It is important to note that while I thank everyone for their candor, I do *not* allow time for a discussion after this question. It's difficult to resist the urge to tell your group what will or will not happen today, but that's not something that you can easily predict. Just know that over the course of the day, you're going to cover a lot of information: material that may either address a specific concern or make it irrelevant.

## Question 2: What factors determine your company's current position within the marketplace? (20 minutes)

The purpose of this question is to get people to think in an in-depth way about the company and to share with the team what they believe sets it apart from the competition. The goal here is to highlight the intrinsic value of what the company has to offer the marketplace in the way of products and services, as well as to hone in on specialized talents within the organization.

Once all responses have been posted on the wall, I then ask if there's anything missing, something someone may have thought of while others were talking. We then take ten minutes or so as a team to discuss the significance of these factors and the role they play in the company's success.

It's always an interesting discussion because I get to see the company through the employees' eyes. And what makes it really cool is that while the team members are more often than not on the same page, there is always that great nugget of insight or perspective that causes you to smile and go "hmm ..." All companies need to stop and think about themselves in this way.

## Question 3: What are the needs of the marketplace? (20 minutes)

This question turns the team's attention to the marketplace. In most organizations, the owners and salespeople have the greatest insight into the market. However, it's always surprising to hear the perspective of supposed backroom personnel.

This question is meant to elicit information on the market's makeup, culture, specific niches, and positive and negative trends, and finally, on the competition. This list should be larger and more in-depth than the one that Question 2 produces, as there are always more areas of opportunity within the market than those that you are currently serving.

Once all responses have been posted on the wall, I again ask if there's anything missing. We then take ten minutes or so as a team to discuss the significance of these factors and the role they play in the company's success, and then we move on to the next step.

## *Question 4: Answering the Scenario. (20 minutes)*

With the team ready to roll, it's finally time to share the Scenario. At this point, I hand a copy of it to each participant and then read it aloud to the group. When finished, I open the floor for a minute or two of clarification questions only—and then I start the timer. This is where the process hits overdrive, as each person gets to unleash their individual creativity.

As the last one to respond, I simply sit back and watch as each team member gets up and tells the rest of the team what we need to do in order to achieve the goals laid out in The Scenario. I navigate this part of the session pretty tightly and allow only a minimum of discussion between responses until everyone is finished. That's when we really begin the dialogue and break down the responses as a group.

After finally presenting my response to the group, I ask everyone to stop and take a look at all of the information posted on the walls. We've done a ton of thinking in a very short period of time, and it's very cool to see all of the collective brainpower plastered along the wall.

Once again, I ask if there's anything missing. By this time, everyone's brain is a bit fatigued, so we break for lunch, where side conversations usually continue. Everyone is now locked into the discussion—and so the next step is to build the plan.

## *Question 5: What is the Plan?*

Here is when we stop working solo and complete the rest of the process as a team. It's time to take all of the information posted on the walls and turn it into a coherent plan. To do this, we have to break all of the material down into smaller pieces.

In order to begin separating the Scenario's answers, we line the wall with five or six blank sheets of paper and title each individually: Sales, Marketing, Operations, and so on. As a team, we then identify those ideas that make the collective cut and place them onto the appropriate sheet of paper. We also begin to identify and list projects within each category. In this case, we listed assignments such as the business/biker posters, book interviews, workshop marketing, client services, and so on. Once the list is complete, we assign leaders to the projects, along with the people and resources needed to assist them. We then agree, as a group, to the projects' order of priority, and we assign start and finish dates to them.

At this point, the group is usually on a roll and in a very positive mood. They believe that everything listed can and will be accomplished exactly when we say it will. In fact, everyone who undertakes this process—whether it's the first time or the fifth—is overly optimistic as to what can really be accomplished. The reality check comes the next day when we walk into the office and have to face our usual challenges. But that's OK. The key thing to remember is that we all now have a sense of urgency about the projects. We simply need to remember that this plan covers the entire year, so not everything can or will be started at once. Some projects will begin immediately and others will start later on. So it's now simply a matter of finding the pace at which we can run as a team.

In order to help determine this rhythm, I take six clean sheets of paper and draw lines down the middle, creating a total of 12 columns. I then title each column with successive months, beginning with the month following this session, to represent our upcoming year. Then, according to start date, I place each of the projects into the corresponding months of the year and take a step back. We now have a pretty clear picture of what our year looks like and can identify the months for which we have overbooked projects or the months with excess capacity.

This look at the upcoming year helps us to put things into a more realistic perspective and better harnesses our "do what it takes" energy. We now understand what every team member is required to do, and by when. We are also fully aware of the order in which things must be accomplished, and why. At this point in the process, any and all compromises are made. We move project dates and shift resources from one priority to another—all in broad daylight for everyone to see and agree to.

This is an important step because the team in most entrepreneurial organizations sits on multiple projects at the same time. By reviewing the flow over the course of a year, the team members better appreciate everyone's start and finish lines, which help them to gauge energy flow, schedule vacations, and manage resources (both human and corporate), thereby ensuring a smoother implementation process.

Once we've completed this discussion, I copy it all down onto a simple Action Item Task Chart and voila—my Tactical Plan is complete. I now have a focus, with the specifics necessary to track what each team member is responsible for on a daily, weekly, and monthly basis. It's a beautiful thing; however, we're not quite finished.

### TASK CHART

| TASK | WORK TO BE DONE | SUPPORT NEEDED | DUE DATE |
|------|-----------------|----------------|----------|
|      |                 |                |          |
|      |                 |                |          |
|      |                 |                |          |
|      |                 |                |          |

## Optional Question: *Why won't it work?*

If we still have time—and aren't completely exhausted by this point—I usually ask the group to come up with situations or obstacles that could prevent us from achieving our goals. The objective here is to predict red flags and perhaps take measures to overcome them; at the very least, we'll become aware of their possibility. It's sort of like knowing on a cross-country road trip that you'll be heading through mountains where there may be a frozen bridge or two. You'll then have your eye out for icy conditions, and you'll know what steps to take if confronted with this challenge.

## Review Question 1: *What result do you want to see at the end of the planning session?*

The last thing I do is point to where the answers to Question 1 are posted and ask each person to review his or her response to that question. The point of this is to make sure that all team members' original goals have been met, or at the very least, to allow them to see why they haven't been. After such a productive day of brainstorming, it's rare that anyone voices any unresolved issues, but if this happens, discuss the matter until you can find a resolution, or set a time when you will do so.

Once this question is reviewed, there's now official buy-in to the plan.

## The Tactics (Work to Be Done)

The tangible results of the Tactical Planning Process are easy to identify. All team members were given the opportunity to voice their wants and priorities for the day. All were provided with the time to openly share their thoughts and opinions about the company and dissect the needs of the marketplace. As leader, I planted a flag as to where the company needed to be 12 months out, but worked side by side with them to build the plan rather than handing it down to them. Along the way, all identified compromises were discussed and agreed to, thereby making implementation much easier.

But what comes out of the Tactical Planning Process isn't just a plan; it's clarity of purpose as well. At the end of the day, we have, as a team, identified and focused on the *work to be done.* And in doing so, the process has accomplished a couple of other very important things.

You've ramped up each team member's overall accountability to both fellow team members and the company by clearly identifying everyone's individual role and responsibilities. All team members now know the level at which they must perform in order for the company to achieve its goals. This knowledge also heightens their personal accountability in another very important way, because it forces them to make a simple business decision: whether to come into work every day and perform at the level necessary for the entire team to succeed. From this point forward, there can be no confusion or half stepping. They are now fully aware of the fact that they have to come to their jobs every single day totally dedicated to the challenge.

Most will gladly accept the challenge and appreciate the clarity, some will need a bit more convincing, and still others will never buy into it. For this last group, it's very clear that this is not a ride they want to take. And that's OK. It's good to know from the start if they're in or out, because if they're feeling overwhelmed now, just think of how they will react when the real pressure hits down the line. Trust me, it's easier to make adjustments now, rather than down the line at some crucial point.

The Tactical Planning Process is also a great way to gauge the leadership within the organization. The different parts of the process offer you the unique opportunity to observe and compare everyone's creativity and leadership skills, which you can then evaluate in relation to the work to be done. I watch the little things to see if my leaders are indeed leading during the planning session. Are they willing and able to engage in candid dialogue, or do they simply wait for my direction? Are they open to new ideas, and do their ideas push the edge and play it safe at the right times?

These observations are important, because this is a team plan, not mine alone. Team members need to take ownership and feel free to run with the work assigned to them. So don't be surprised if you see new leaders emerging in your mind after completing the Tactical Planning Session. Because as one of my mentors, Frank Mitchell, once told me, "You never know what you've got until you watch it."

## Tactical Planning Case Study: One CEO's Lesson

Jane was the CEO of a 10-year-old electronics repair depot that was experiencing enormous triple-digit growth after having acquired two new national clients. She desperately needed to map out a method for handling the company's growth for the next three years, so we pulled her management team together for a Tactical Planning Session.

Jane's team consisted of five people who'd been with her since day one, and one recent hire. The roles and responsibilities of the long-term employees had grown in concert with the company, leaving them with little, if any, formal management experience outside of the company to draw on. This is where the new team member came in: Jane had recognized a glaring weakness in the area of operations leadership and had hired an experienced (and highly paid) director of operations 60 days prior to our session.

Jane and I both viewed her new director of operation's short length of time with the organization as a plus for the planning session, because a new set of eyes looking into a company is always a good thing. Her expectations of him were further fueled by the fact that he'd directed the operations of an organization three times the size of hers and appeared to be transitioning into the company nicely.

However, during the entire session, we noticed that his responses were shallow and based more on what he'd read in the latest business book than on solid production experience. He struggled to offer concrete tactics to address the challenges faced within his department and was clearly outshined by the others. To say that this did not go unnoticed by Jane or her team would be an understatement. His lack of contribution was so glaring that as the day wore on, the rest of the team simply stopped engaging him and often cut him off when speaking. I found it nearly impossible to facilitate him back into the discussion.

The day's positive takeaway was that—aside from the director of operations—Jane's team performed at a very high level and we ended up with an excellent plan. At the end of the meeting, Jane asked me to wait and speak with her, because there was a question she needed answered. Once everyone left the room, she looked at me and said, as more of a statement than a question, "He's not going to make it, is he?" To which I replied, "I don't think so." She then revealed the number of dollars spent recruiting him, as well as the moving expenses incurred, and asked my opinion on what she should do.

My answer was straightforward. I said, "If your gut instinct is that he's not a fit, then it's not a question of *if* you're

*(continued)*

going to replace him, but a question of *when*. So the sooner you reconcile this in your mind, the better off your team will be moving forward." Jane agonized over her decision for another month before finally releasing him. Her company went on not only to handle those new clients, but grow into one of the largest players in her industry.

Although Jane ended up dismissing her new director of operations, the point here is *not* that you are in danger of losing key personnel during the Tactical Planning Process. The real danger lies in not knowing that you have someone in a key role who simply doesn't fit. Not only do you and the rest of the organization need to know *now* if it's a bad fit, but the person who's no longer suitable for the position needs to know now, as well. It's unfair to subject someone to the pain and pressure of a role that's inappropriate for his or her talents.

I always say that water seeks its own level, meaning that in the right environment, your team members will either rise or sink to their talent level. This is a good thing for both you and your team to recognize and understand. As you and your organization continue to grow, so should your team, and the best way to gauge this growth is to compare their talents to a workable plan. You are then better able to identify the gaps in their capabilities and close them, if possible.

A great planning session should be simple and painless. Properly done, it will be something your team members look forward to, because it becomes their forum for an in-depth discussion in which they agree to and organize their tactics. The end result will have your team members on the same page, more energized and focused on the goal because they will have identified the who, what, and when of growing your business. We'll address the how and why in the next chapter.

## Road Rules

- Do *not* skip Questions 1 through 3 and go directly to the Scenario. Your plan will suffer if you do.
- Having each team member individually answer the questions is the key to a great session.
- Whenever possible, take the session off-site and away from the day-to-day routine so you can focus on possibilities.
- You have a plan if it contains the following:
  - Clearly defined roles
  - Clearly delegated authority and responsibility
  - Systems and processes
  - Agreed-upon reporting structure with dates

---

*You can access my free tools to help you Plan Your Ride, along with detailed instructions, on my web site at www.BikersGuidetoBusiness.com.*

 CHAPTER 13

# The Work to Be Done

Whenever I—or one of my clients—is faced with a seemingly overwhelming issue, I focus on one thing: the work to be done. While this includes overall goals and objectives, it really focuses on the day-to-day tasks that I need to complete in order to "get there." I've found that when clearly defined and agreed to, the work to be done drives behavior, ramps up accountability, and encourages teamwork.

I've been approached hundreds of times to present some sort of team-building workshop. My response is always the same; though I'll gladly do that, my talk will focus more intently on work than on personality. I explain that we'll not hold hands, catch people as they fall off logs, or climb ropes like kindergartners. Instead, I believe that a team is built around a mission and a purpose. To be sure, those other, more touchy-feely workshops will have everyone feeling good about each other—for a while. But over the long term, they won't earn you one damned dime. Because this is business, and business is about getting the company from here to there quickly and profitably. And a group becomes a team when, over time, they execute the company's mission effectively and successfully. Does everyone like each other the entire time? Is it always warm and fuzzy? Hell no, building a great company is hard work. It's also incredibly demanding work. Any great mission has these distinct elements:

- An unambiguous vision and direction for the company
- Lucid, identified goals for the group and for each person
- A clearly stated strategy on how to achieve these goals
- Established lines of communication
- Opportunities for both corporate and personal growth

Fall short in any one area, and the team will struggle. I'm not saying you won't eventually get to where you want to be, but the journey will not be easy.

Regarding the importance of the work to be done and why, I'm often asked, "What about the people?" Well, I learned a long time ago from a college professor and confirmed through experience that if you focus on performance, personalities take care of themselves.

Think in terms of a successful sports team. Each player has a role and job to do. If the players do not perform well, then the team either struggles or loses altogether. The really good teams focus on the role of each player when making personnel decisions. Indeed, this often comes across as cold and harsh, especially when the team cuts someone who's performed well in the past. But the focus here is on the future and winning, and on doing so in a very public way. The external pressure is intense, because the fans are watching. And they only know and care about one thing: the final score. The fans don't know that the player's spouse is sick or that the player was up with a sick child all night, which had a negative impact on performance. And they don't really care, because regardless of outside distractions, the players have a job to do and their accomplishments, or lack thereof, are clearly visible to everyone watching.

However, I'm told that this is not necessarily the case in business. Our performance is not that visible and not as cut-and-dried. And to that I say, "Huh?" Business is the biggest win–or–lose game there is. Second place is simply the first-place loser. You may not be showing your stuff to fans on a field or a court, but the show that you put on is just as important. You either get the gig—and make the sale—or you do not. There's no in-between.

And although you may think there aren't that many people watching, I beg to differ. All your team members are watching. They know who is pulling his or her weight and who isn't. Certainly they will pitch in and support others when necessary, but that's an exception. Over time, any team members who are doing another's share of work will start to resent that person and eventually diminish their own labor if nothing is done about it. It's the old "weakest link in the chain" situation, and if you're noticing mediocre efforts coming from your team, you may need to cull the herd of nonperformers.

That being said, the insidious issue here is that it's not always easy to determine who is shirking responsibility. It may be someone who, on the surface, seems to be putting forth effort, but falls short when it comes to results. You like this person's spirit and hard work, and you try your best to provide help, but the performance is just not there. So you turn to your winners and push them harder or ask them to do more. You go home at night feeling good because you've attempted to salvage this person, but your best performers go home feeling like crap because they had to pull more than their share of the load. They sit at home stewing or gripe about it at happy hour and wonder when you're going to wake up and see that person for what he or she is—dead weight.

When this occurs, one of two things is bound to happen: Either your best players' performance will start to slide (after all, it's a proven fact that you accept mediocrity) or they will quit from the pressure. My experience has shown that top performers don't quit good companies—they quit bad managers. Think about that the next time you lose a great employee. The person will say something nice on their way out like "No, it's great here. I just received another offer that's too good to refuse." But that, my friend, is the epitome of the "It's not you, it's me" euphemism; all the while, both you and your departing employee know that it's really *you*.

To avoid losing these winning employees, you need to be proactive. If the nonperformers have been onboard for any length of time, then it's obvious that the problem lies with them and not you. Yes, as entrepreneurs we'll second-guess ourselves to death, wondering if we've given them enough training or tools. Stop! Unless you are a minister, you are *not* in the salvation business. Your company is all about performance and nothing else, or as it was put to me one day, "I don't want to hear about how hard they worked; I just want to know what they've done." After all, that's probably the only thing that your customers care about.

Probably the best and most extreme example of the importance of worker performance is the experience of my good friend Ken. The founder and CEO of a 90-store operation, Ken has learned some tough lessons about people in growing his company. Ken saw his company grow rapidly early on, only to crash later in a rather dramatic fashion. After exhaustive research as to why, he came to understand that his growth had outstripped the capabilities of his employees. And to his credit, he didn't just go about finding more experienced people—he went about finding the *right* people.

Ken researched what the most profitable companies were doing, incorporated those lessons into his hiring and training process, and customized the process to his needs. Now, years later, his company is undergoing massive growth and has become the most profitable in his industry by a wide margin.

I don't tell this story to highlight Ken's hiring process, but rather to discuss the standards and accountability he attached to it. With a good process in place, Ken knows with certainty that when he hires the right type of people, invests in their training, and provides the proper resources, they will produce a precise amount of revenue. Taking his employees' time on the job and experience into account, he knows what to expect in terms of performance and profitability, and he rigorously holds each of his employees to those standards.

These standards were never more evident than in a conversation that Ken and I recently had. One of his top regional managers, who had been number one for three years running, had hit a slump. After 60 days, Ken called him into the office to discuss the reasons. Personal problems were to blame, and while Ken was compassionate, he knew that he had a company to run. He also knew that the rest of the company was watching.

Now, understand that Ken takes very, *very* good care of his people. He pays the highest wages and has the best bonus plan in the industry. His managers also enjoy the smallest span of control, meaning that instead of overseeing the usual 9 to 10 stores, they manage a maximum of 5. This allows them to keep a closer eye on things and is one of the reasons that Ken's business is so profitable.

So, with that in mind, Ken looked at the regional manager and said, "I'm sending you home for 30 days to fix your problem and also to decide if you can come back and perform at the level the company needs you to. And while you're gone, I'll be thinking about whether or not it's appropriate, in light of your letting the team down, to have you come back."

Wow, here he is, Ken's top performing manager for three years running, and he had a mere 60-day slump—and was benched immediately. I would be willing to bet that 99.9 percent of all CEOs would never have even bothered to have that conversation with an employee, much less bench him or her. And as you might guess, the manager returned after the 30 days with promises of improved performance, but Ken stood his ground and let him go.

That surprised even me, but Ken made his rationale clear: "I had to look at the team as a whole, and the risk of him coming back and not performing was too great. My gut told me that his head was no longer in the game—so why put off the inevitable? I have the best trained, most aggressive, and most successful team in the business. This means that I also had to worry about eroding my message about performance, and I decided that keeping him on was simply not worth it. Besides, my bench is deep, and the person who replaced him is taking that region to places that the other guy simply could not."

I know that many of the people reading this will find Ken's dismissal of his regional manager fairly extreme, and it most certainly is. However, that doesn't make it *wrong*. In fact, our shocked reaction shows how far we've fallen in terms of defining excellence, and highlights our willingness to accept mediocre performance. This is something we should never accept. And the "work to be done" philosophy doesn't just focus on overall personnel performance. It also addresses the proper placement of your people within the organization, and thus may be the most important principle of all. Having clarity on what needs to be done allows you to better determine whether the people doing the work are the best ones to do so—at *all* levels.

## Leadership Case Study: It Runs in the Family

A few years ago, I was contacted by the youngest of three brothers who had jointly inherited a successful company from their father. They faced a classic problem. When the father left, he did what most businesspeople do in such a case. He gave the lead position of CEO to Walt, the oldest son. The issue here was that Walt was clearly in over his head, having recently gone through a divorce. He had also essentially divorced himself from the daily leadership of the company, putting middle brother Sam in the position of daily manager and leader. Also, Walt was not comfortable making significant decisions, because for the past year he'd relegated himself to running a distant branch of the company 100 miles away. This caused a great deal of confusion not only within the ranks of the company, but with customers outside of the organization as well.

Both Sam and the youngest brother, Terry, also a leader in the company, recognized the danger in allowing the current situation to continue. They were desperate to change the official leadership structure, but wanted to do so in a way that would salvage their relationship as brothers. However, this would prove to be far trickier than anticipated. The night I flew in to meet with the brothers, Walt blew off our dinner in order to take his girlfriend to a rock concert, leaving Sam and Terry beside themselves with frustration. They'd flown in someone from halfway across the country to help the three of them work through an increasingly critical issue, and the third member of their team had abandoned them in favor of a night out on the town with his girlfriend!

We did use our time at dinner to discuss their primary goal: to fix the top-level structure of the company. Both agreed that Sam should be CEO because Walt had essentially abdicated the role over a year ago. That was the easy part. I was there because of my experience in helping other family businesses restructure without destroying the family. This was the clear mission here: Fix the company while keeping the brothers' relationship intact. It was clear that Sam and Terry loved Walt and needed to work it all out in a way that would cause minimal conflict.

*(continued)*

I assured them I'd do my best and then turned the conversation toward the company. I asked them where they thought it needed to be three to five years down the line. We spent the remainder of dinner discussing its positioning and goals, all of which would serve as the foundation to our discussion the next day.

The following day we met off-site, far away from the distractions of the company. Walt was late, of course, but not overly so. I began by laying the ground rules for the day and emphasized that this was about the *good of the business*—and only that. All personal issues were out of bounds and would be discussed only after our business was complete.

I then opened the floor for a 30-minute discussion in which the brothers could feel free to put on the table any of the issues that had led us to that point. The discussion was frank and candid, with many personal jabs taken along the way. At this point, I allowed the brothers their jabs because I knew it would be impossible for them to keep it impersonal; after all, they *were* brothers.

This was also the first time I began to hear from Walt, who seemed a tad tired from the previous night's festivities. Without going into too much detail, it was immediately clear to me that he was on a different wavelength. Ego is a strong driver and although Walt knew he wasn't actively running the company, he clearly didn't want to give up the title of CEO to his little brother.

At that point, I introduced the Scenario of where the company needed to be three to five years in the future, based on my conversation with Terry and Sam the previous evening. As a group, we discussed and honed it into a crystal-clear vision to which everyone agreed. I then began breaking it down into projects—literally, the work to be done—and had them assign their individual functional responsibilities associated with each project. About two hours into the discussion, it was becoming very clear who the number-one leader of the organization was, and more importantly, *should* be. All top-level duties naturally fell to Sam, since he either fulfilled them already or they logically fell within his areas of responsibility.

It was at that moment during the meeting that Sam threw a verbal jab at Walt, outwardly wondering why he didn't hold the title of CEO. Walt responded in a surprisingly cocky manner and proclaimed that "Titles don't mean a f'ing thing to me, and you can have the damned title for all I care." To which I quickly jumped in and said, "Done! Thanks, Walt."

I then immediately turned to Sam and said, "Now that that's settled, how do we move forward and announce it to the company?" Terry immediately read what I was doing and began to chime in with ideas and suggestions, leaving Walt to sit there and wonder what the heck had just happened. I think that Walt had fully expected a verbal joust with Sam, but when I literally ripped the title out of midair and handed it to Sam, any chance of that was ended.

We spent the remainder of the meeting preparing for Sam's announcement to the management team during our conference the following day. Walt remained in a state of semishock for the rest of the day and eventually exploded over dinner, leaving the restaurant before even eating his meal. I hurriedly walked him out and asked if he'd do me a favor and pick me up the next day to drive me to the meeting. He agreed. I returned to the table, where Sam and Terry were wondering aloud if we'd done the right thing. After all, they proclaimed, they'd rather lose the business than their brother.

*(continued)*

I assured them—with more hope than certainty—that things would work out the next day, and they did. I used my time in the car with Walt that morning to have an intense 40-minute conversation (my real reason for needing a ride to the meeting), in which he finally accepted the reality of his situation. He had known that it was coming for months, and settling on the details lifted a huge weight from his shoulders. The only thing left for him to do now was to find his true place within the company, beyond that of an owner.

Unfortunately, I returned a few months later to lead the entire management team through two days of Tactical Planning and found them still struggling with Walt's lack of productivity. However, the good news was that the company was clearly flourishing under Sam's control. The management team was no longer confused as to who the leader was, and they were hitting on all cylinders.

Walt left the company a few years later; he never could seem to find his true place. But the brothers' relationship remains intact and as strong as ever, because Walt, Sam, and Terry were able to separate their personal lives from their business by focusing on the work to be done. After all, in the end, successful performance is the one thing that should *never* be compromised.

 # Road Rules

- Focus on performance and not personality—everything revolves around the work.
- Get the right talent in the right place.
- People are happiest when they are in the right job and perform effectively.

 CHAPTER 14

# Communication

## The Fuel of High Performance

A group's ability to achieve high performance when executing the Tactical Plan is hinged on its ability to communicate *well*. On a long motorcycle ride, we do this with hand signals or group discussions at fuel stops. In business, the main way to do this is to hold meetings.

But let's face it: No one likes to meet.

Walk into any company and ask about the effectiveness of the meetings, and chances are that you'll hear mutterings about wastes of time. However, there's no way around it; *you have to talk*. The key is how—and why.

In this chapter, I'll cover the three main meeting types, what to watch out for, and how and when to use them, because all meetings are not created equal. But before I go there, consider and answer the following questions:

- Do you consider meetings to be a necessary evil?
- Do you and your colleagues see meetings as wastes of time that are only called to discuss the latest fire raging across the organization?

- Do meetings of 10 turn into a conversation between 2 or 3 people—leaving the rest of the team members to wonder why they're even there?
- Do you end up in the proverbial ditch, having veered so far off track at a meeting that no one remembers the reason you got together in the first place?

If you're like 99 out of 100 companies, you answered yes to one or all of these questions. And that's OK, because over the course of my career I've come to understand that the reason we hate meetings and avoid them like the plague is that few of us were ever taught the proper how and why of business meetings in the first place. Think back on the original training that you received when you first entered the business world. Did anyone bother to sit you down and teach you how to meet? I'd wager the answer is no, which is why most professionals and companies tend to struggle in this area. Unfortunately, the usual method of communicating a plan in most companies is to simply hand it out to all employees who are present at a meeting and expect that they will be able to implement it with little or no allowance for follow-up communication. After all, the plan's been clearly stated. What else could they possibly need in order to get it done?

That's a dangerous assumption to make, and one that often leads to the Tragedy of Strategy I discussed in Chapter 5. The reality is that once you determine your tactics, you have to implement them through a series of meetings, because it's within these meetings that real Navigation takes place. You need to spend time keeping your team on track and ensuring that they communicate with each other. Carefully designed meetings also have other benefits, such as one-on-one coaching, mentoring, and teaching employees those ever-elusive critical thinking skills. I know you're probably thinking, "Hell, I don't have enough time in the day as it is. The last thing I have is time to hold their hands." But the bottom line here is that your level of performance will be determined by the extent to which you and your colleagues embrace these meetings.

I believe that there are only three types of meetings in any company, and believe it or not, you're most likely already attending them. The question is whether you're using them the right way and at the right time. They are

- Group meetings
- Cruise-by meetings
- One-on-one meetings

I'll give a detailed description of each one.

## Group Meetings

I define a *group meeting* as one in which three or more people come together to discuss one or several topics. These meetings are necessary and important, and are designed to get information out to a lot of people at one time. They should be global in nature and should not drop below the 5,000-foot level; in other words, they should not get bogged down in too much detail and small talk. The problem is that they rarely, if ever, progress the way they should.

How many times have you walked into a meeting with no agenda that is led by a talking head who is forcing everyone to listen while he rants about the latest thing that's ticking him off? And how often have you walked into a meeting with 10 attendees that turns into an exchange among 2 or 3 people in which the entire conversation focuses solely on them, leaving the rest of the group to wonder when the hell it's going to be over. Eventually, in either meeting, everyone will begin to mentally check out, one by one, or the meeting will end up in the weeds and turn into a gripe and bitch session where nothing is accomplished. Sound familiar?

I remember beginning a gig with a client who held a weekly meeting to discuss production and issues. During my first interviews with the managers, I asked about the effectiveness of this meeting. Three out of five immediately asked me to "save them."

They all agreed that the meetings were necessary; unfortunately, the meetings were always driven by the hot topic of the week because the managers never created an agenda. And the hot topic for the past three weeks had been "Who needs to clean out the refrigerator?"

Has this happened to you? Come on now, be honest. We've all attended those types of meetings. Just replace *refrigerator* with something else, and chances are you've been there. And you have probably, at some point in time, even conducted that meeting yourself. After all, it's *your* meeting, you're pissed, and by gosh, you're gonna vent about it. You have the power, and so you do it.

Unfortunately, you're also blowing incredible amounts of productivity, time, and most importantly, focus. So how do you get those group meetings on track?

It all starts with your Tactical Plan, because the reason you're meeting in the first place is to track and discuss its implementation. To ensure forward motion, there must be, at the very least, monthly follow-up meetings in which the people who are heading up the key categories come together in one room to talk about their progress. My recommendation is to hold them weekly at first, because you can always lengthen the time between meetings if you feel that it's appropriate. But do yourself a big favor and start off more stringently, because it's easier to loosen the reins than to tighten them.

A key point to keep in mind is that this is a meeting where *you* need to gain insight as to how your team is working on the plan, so *you* have the role as facilitator. This means that your participation is limited to keeping the conversations on track, but your role should not hinder your comprehension. Set the time, start on time, end on time, and hold it to an hour! Starting late both penalizes those who arrive on time and ensures that your meetings will begin to slide to a point where you find them beginning increasingly later—and eventually affecting the rest of your day's schedule.

Your agenda should be simple and focus on how the Tactical Plan is fitting into your team's daily business life, and the meeting should be designed to accurately track the team's progress. During the meeting, the interactions between team members should be brief and to the point, and remain at a high level without going into too much detail, unless you are discussing a specific issue and formulating a solution. You'll need to discipline yourself and the team to end on time; you'll soon recognize the side conversations that need to be quickly ended and saved for a separate meeting at another time or, as we call it, an offline interaction.

On the next page is a sample agenda upon which you can model your own team meetings. As you become more aware of your own needs and patterns, you can fine-tune this document; it is simply a jumping-off point.

Now, let's break each section of the meeting down.

## Section I: Team Updates

The best way to direct the conversation and prevent it from becoming one that's led by a single talking head is to have each team member complete the Update form (see page 146) before the meeting and review it with the other members during the meeting. (Each team member should distribute copies of his or her own form to everyone at the meeting.) This form is designed to allow each member to quickly discuss what has happened in his or her world since the last meeting. The team members go around the table one by one, allowing for minimal questions, and discuss the following items:

---

# Management Team
## Meeting Agenda

Date: _____          Time: _____

I. **Team Updates**
   (see Update form on page 146.)
   - Manager 1
   - Manager 2
   - Manager 3

II. **Issue Discussion**
   - Issue 1
   - Issue 2

III. **Miscellaneous Ancillary Items**
   - Item 1
   - Item 2

IV. **Conclusion**
   - Date of next meeting
   - Dates for one-on-one meetings
   - Assigned tasks
     - Task 1
     - Task 2
     - Task 3

---

### *What is the best thing to happen to you since the last meeting?*

This item gives the team member a chance to either toot their own horn or that of one of their employees. It lets them start the meeting in a positive way. On the flip side, if certain team members have nothing good to report, you may want to meet with that individual later to discuss the reasons in depth.

### *What are your top priorities? What are you currently focused on?*

The responses to this item allow you to better understand each colleague's priorities and make any necessary adjustments. It also helps you to better grasp what support and resources may be needed to accomplish the tasks.

### *What have you accomplished since we last met?*

This item gives you the chance to recognize any crossed finish lines. Too often in business, we complete one task and jump right into the other without savoring a sense of accomplishment and stopping to celebrate.

### *What issues are getting in your way?*

This is where your team members bring forth the challenges facing them as they go through their days. This gives each person a chance to understand what's happening in other departments and helps each team member determine how and when to chip in and help.

### *What is the best thing you want to have happen by the next meeting?*

This part is fairly self-explanatory: Your team members identify the tasks and goals they want to accomplish before the next meeting. This should help both you and your teammates hone in on each person's top priority.

Give each participant five minutes to cover the update, with minimal questions and interruptions from the rest of the team. When you think in these terms, you will be able to see exactly how long the meeting should last; for example, if you have six people in the meeting, it will take about 30 minutes to complete the update portion of the meeting.

Keep in mind that during the first few meetings, you may struggle to simply get through the updates. That's completely

# Management Team
## Update

Name: _____          Date: _____

**Best thing to happen to you since the last meeting:**
_____

**Top priorities:**
- _____
- _____
- _____
- _____
- _____
- _____

**Accomplishments:**
- _____
- _____
- _____
- _____
- _____
- _____

**Miscellaneous issues:**
- _____
- _____
- _____
- _____
- _____
- _____

**Best thing you want to have happen by the next meeting:**
_____

normal; you are setting a new baseline and establishing a new method for sharing information. Over time, the updates will move more quickly, and you'll find that each team member will take, on average, less than five minutes for the update, thereby allowing you more time for tackling issues.

## Section II: Issues

Never—let me say this again—*never* tackle more than two issues per meeting. Ideally, you should only tackle one. Why? I'm sure you've attended meetings with 10 items on the agenda where all you managed was to briefly touch on each of them. Skimming topics like this leaves everyone frustrated and wanting more, and if you do explore every item in depth, your meeting ends up lasting four hours and blowing everyone's schedule. Remember that in this ADD-esque world, you're really pushing the envelope of comprehension and attention at an hour, and you've definitely reached the point of diminishing returns at the 90-minute mark. So in order to keep meetings under these time limits, you must get the key information regarding any issues out on the table quickly and manage the major time thief of all meetings: questions. Don't get me wrong; I love questions and I know that they're critical to group understanding. But you must find a way to manage them.

The most effective way to tackle issues is to first have a team member present them in writing using the *Three Ws of Critical Thinking*. This format serves an important purpose. By requiring a team member to clearly present an issue in five minutes or less, the format compels the presenter to essentially resolve the issue prior to the meeting. If team members use the format correctly, they are presenting their issues for only three reasons: to determine if they've missed anything, to check their thinking, and to inform the rest of the team what their actions will be.

# Three Ws of Critical Thinking

**What is the issue?**

(This can be addressed in one or two sentences.)

- Explain how and why you have reached this crossroads. Include (where appropriate) the following:
  - Brief history leading up to the current situation
  - Resources and limitations
  - Financial impact of the issue
  - Potential long-term effects and pros and cons
  - Miscellaneous relevant data
- Indicate the focus of the issue (strategic, financial, operational, or organizational).
- Incorporate the measurable result of successfully addressing the issue.

**What are the options?**

(These are the methods that you are exploring and evaluating to address the issue.)

- Brainstorm new options when preparing this blueprint.
- List several different options. Include those with obvious pitfalls; perhaps there are ways to make them work.
- Indicate the choice you feel is best, and why.

**What do you recommend?**

(Describe the corrective action you want to implement.)

- Include the following:
  - Additional research planned
  - Timetable for achieving goal
  - Priority level of issue
- Include a detailed plan, if available, for review by team.
- **Note:** The specifics of an action plan may be developed after getting team feedback.

Make sure that all members of the team receive a written summary of each presentation, so that they can follow along and make notations while the presenting member reads it to the group.

After the presenter has addressed the Three Ws, you can then facilitate the discussion of the issue according to the Feedback Guidelines (see page 150).

The process is as follows:

- The presenting member reads the issue to the group.
- Open the floor for questions only—do not allow any feedback or questions disguised as feedback.
- Once all questions have been asked and answered, have all members go quiet for three minutes to record their feedback.
- One by one, have all members read their feedback to the presenting member, who must stay quiet the entire time while taking notes on what each member is suggesting.
- Once all members have given their feedback, open the floor to discussion. The presenting member can now ask further questions in order to build upon any ideas.
- Finally, ask the presenting member what suggestions he or she heard but does *not* plan to use to resolve the issue. This gives you a clear picture of the member's future actions and an idea of what actions and results to hold him or her accountable for.

The benefit of the Three Ws and the Feedback Guidelines is that you are establishing a method of critical thinking and problem solving for your team. By working together, team members begin to better understand the challenges facing them individually and as a team. The process fosters unity and professionalism as you drive your plan forward.

# Feedback Guidelines

## *Presenting Member*

- Read the Three Ws for your issue quickly and efficiently.
- Answer all questions in a clear and concise manner.
- Use the quiet time to revisit your issue and think about the areas of feedback you are interested in receiving.
- Listen to the feedback from each team member *without comment*. Write down your thoughts and make note of any comments you want to make about the feedback.
- Be open-minded; avoid getting defensive.
- After all members have offered their insights and questions, it's OK to challenge and discuss the pertinent feedback you have received.
- Summarize the ideas you heard that have the most impact. State the action you will be taking as a result of the feedback.


## *Responding Members*

- Listen carefully to the Three Ws. Solicit any additional information you need to offer feedback.
- During quiet time, write down feedback for all ideas.
- Break down the individual areas of the blueprint:

    **Issue:** *Is it the right goal? Is the member focusing on a symptom rather than a real issue? Has the member identified resources and limitations? Is there an area that needs additional research? Is anything missing?*
    **Options:** *Are these the only options? Think outside the box.*
    **Recommendation:** *What should the member do first? What follow-up information will you need in subsequent meetings?*

- Also consider the following questions:
  - *What are the long-term effects of this issue, both positive and negative?*
  - *How does this issue affect the product, employees, and customers?*
  - *What is the emotional side of this issue for the member?*
- Communicate your comments briefly and feel free to share common experiences.
- Reveal *all* feedback, even if you are echoing another member and even if you see an obvious shortcoming to it. Someone else may see a way to make it work.
- Listen to the members before you and build on their ideas.
- Share any and all additional ideas during the discussion phase.

## Section III: Miscellaneous Ancillary Items

This is where ancillary items of interest are introduced, time permitting. This discussion may result in a future issue or other items of note, such as absences, trade shows, and so on, that may affect the team in the future.

## Section IV: Concluding the Meeting

I cannot tell you how many meetings I attend where it ends simply with everyone getting up and leaving the room without proper closure. In order to ensure that everyone is on the same page I use the following tactics:

- Take the last five minutes of the meeting to recap what was discussed.
- Set or review the future meeting date to ensure full attendance.

- Schedule any one-on-one meetings that may have resulted from the discussion.
- Review all assigned tasks.

Remember that productive meetings are run with a production mind-set. The meeting must be established with a desired result in mind, and it should produce clearly defined roles and agreed-upon targets with *dates attached*. Otherwise, it's just a coffee klatch. So follow your agenda, control the questions, kill side conversations, and at the end, recap. Then turn your face into the wind and ride!

## Cruise-By Meetings

*Cruise-by meetings* are the most overused and least effective way to communicate in business today. In the name of efficiency, you drop in, or you cruise by, a colleague's office. The conversation usually starts with "Got a sec?" or "Quick question for you . . ." In any case, it's always an interruption to the person receiving the unexpected visit.

These meetings are without structure and tend to foster poor communication because they are rushed, spontaneous, and unplanned. You are always either interrupting someone or being interrupted. This type of interaction is subject to hit-or-miss comprehension and is the single greatest cause of things falling through the cracks in any organization.

Think about it: The people you interrupt are 10 minutes into a 20-minute project. You say, "Hey, got a second?" And what happens? First, their focus is broken. Second, by the time they begin to engage in your conversation, you're two or three sentences into your topic—and all the while, they're nodding their head and giving you the impression that they understand exactly what you're saying. But in reality, they simply want you to finish and leave so they can get back to what they were doing.

You are asking them to immediately digest and respond to something that, depending on their personality, they probably need more time to absorb. Sixty seconds later, you either have your answer or you've successfully passed the hot potato and everything's fine, right? Wrong!

Or you decide to sit down, settle in, and discuss the matter at hand—and it becomes a BS session. After your initial 60-second issue, you then break into another discussion about something going on within the company. All the while, you're piling more work on the people you interrupted. You've heightened their anxiety, because they now have even more work to do and aren't making any sort of progress on the project they were focusing on. Also note that the 20-minute project they were 10 minutes into when interrupted will now take them at least *another* 20 minutes to complete, now that their focus has been broken.

Take the number of employees you have, and multiply that by 10 minutes. That's the amount of productivity you lose each day in your company by trying to save time with these cruise-by meetings, and that's if they only happen once per person!

Certainly, cruise-by meetings are necessary in every organization. I understand that—it's the real world. Just understand that these interactions lack depth and should therefore be limited to time-sensitive yes-or-no questions or brief points of clarification. *Never* use them for creative or strategic thinking. If that's what you need, then either send an e-mail or stop by and simply ask your colleague when the two of you can schedule a time to meet (and have a time in mind to make it easy). This way, both of you can walk in with clear minds that are open to the discussion, and you will both be better equipped to focus on the issue at hand.

## One-on-One Meetings

*One-on-one meetings* are the least utilized yet most important type of meeting in business today. Why are they so vital? Because they're where depth happens. These are the meetings that convey the why behind the how. They help you understand the whole person, and foster a strong business connection. These intimate meetings are where the real coaching and truly crucial conversations take place. However, these kinds of meetings are usually held infrequently and therefore done poorly. For one-on-one meetings to be effective, they *must* be held on a consistent basis. Otherwise, they will have more of a negative than a positive effect.

Consider why you usually call someone into your office to meet one-on-one. More often than not, it's either to discuss a mistake they've made or load them up with more work. In either case, it becomes the "principal's office" and causes one of two reactions: fight or flight. And all of this fosters the "green room effect." For those of you not familiar with the green room effect, the term refers to a study in which researchers placed a dog in a blue room where it received water, then a brown room in which it received food, and then a green room, where it was hit with a bright light and loud noise. It didn't take the dog long to learn not to walk into green rooms.

If your team is to develop, and to trust you and understand what you are doing and why, then these one-on-ones are *critical*. These meetings allow you to get to know all the individual members of your team and, in doing so, understand where they fit in your overall plans. These meetings give you a better chance of setting up these team members for success.

I'll share an example of the power of the one-on-ones. I work with a high-performance, production-based organization. Of all its pressure-packed departments, project management is the most intense; everything either comes through or revolves around this team. The manager is a no-nonsense woman whose standards of performance and excellence are matched only by the owners. She's tough but fair, and is the widely recognized hard-ass of the company.

A couple of years ago, we were reviewing turnover rates at the end of the year. We noticed a 25 percent turnover in one department and 40 percent in another, and then we got to the project management department. It had a zero percent turnover for two years running! And to top it off, the person this manager had replaced was still working in the department and now reporting to her.

Now, as an observer of business, I was naturally interested in this phenomenon, so I sat with the manager to find out her secret. I asked how she did it, and she looked at me and said, "Dwain, it's simple. I took your advice and hold *weekly* one-on-one meetings with my people. I have 13 people on my team, so I know that I'll have to devote 10 to 13 hours each week to these interactions. But these meetings are sacred. The team members all know their assigned times and come in prepared with their Update forms. We discuss their—and my—performance. I pat them on the back when it's good and ask them what happened when it's not. I also ask them what I did or didn't do that may have contributed to their missing the mark.

"Over time, it's become a more casual conversation and one where we talk about family and weekend stuff, but it's always centered on the work to be done. I need to know when they're having a hard time with something outside of the company and how I can take steps to support them. It helps me do my job better, so they can do theirs better. We no longer look at it as a chore, but instead really miss it if we ever need to reschedule. It's the most productive time I spend the entire week."

Think of what this woman told me: "It's the most productive time I spend the entire week." Then think about zero percent turnover and high-performance employees. Pretty amazing results for your average meeting, huh?

Make it easy on yourself and use the Update form to establish a basis for your conversation. It keeps your discussions focused and also further establishes, at all levels, the communication structure for the company. I cannot emphasize the importance of these interactions enough; the one-on-one meeting is *key* to breaking the "do what it takes" syndrome many managers suffer from. It allows you to get things done through other people and to have them grow before your eyes—all very quickly.

**Note:** When determining the frequency of your one-on-one or group meetings, you must be aware of the time effect. If you meet with someone or a group weekly, you will be discussing two weeks in time: the past week and the upcoming week. If you meet once a month, then you're dealing with two months in time; if you meet once a quarter, it's a six-month view. Get the picture?

That's why meetings are so important; depending on how fast your company moves, a lot can happen in a week, two weeks, or a month. Therefore, it's imperative that you communicate with your team in a timely manner.

 **Road Rules**

- All great business meetings include a clear goal and are conducted in a way that ensures everyone thoroughly understands it.
- At the end of the meeting, let your team members know what you expect them to do to meet the goal, and by when.
- Let your team members know what they can expect of *you,* and by when.

*You can access my free tools to help you better Communicate, along with detailed instructions, on my web site at www.BikersGuidetoBusiness.com.*

CHAPTER 15

# Harnessing the Power of the Pack

One of my favorite truths is the maxim that *"Business is easy ... until you add people."* If you give one person a particular task, he or she is in total control. However, adding more people into the mix doesn't necessarily grant them control; the most that they can hope for is influence. Therefore, to a degree, every company is dysfunctional, simply because it involves multiple people with competing agendas that eventually lead to conflict and then to poor performance.

For example, a company of 50 employees has, on any given day, around 200 individual agendas waiting to run it off the road or, at the very least, slow it down. Family obligations, internal personnel issues, and vendor or client problems can easily add up and hover over any business like a rain cloud. Everyone has these challenges, and you can't prevent them. Therefore, the only way to maintain direction and focus is to accept the fact that the organization is inherently flawed, and work accordingly. What follows are a few of the ways I get teams to *harness the power of the pack* so they can consistently perform at the highest level.

# Team Building

Any discussion about dysfunction within an organization comes with a negative connotation. However, dysfunction is simply a barometer to measure how well the people in a company mesh to create the overall culture of the organization. It took me a long time to understand this reality; before figuring it out, I spent years searching in vain for the silver bullet that would put everything on track. There's been book after book written about the notion of team building, and even an entire industry built around it. Each tool comes complete with the promise of turning anyone's dysfunctional team into one big happy family. And some of the concepts would be funny—if they weren't so worthless.

There are consultants that will take you and your team out into the woods to climb on logs or up 10-foot poles so that, one by one, you can each fall backwards into your teammates' arms and they will (hopefully) catch you in order to build trust. Or the consultants will separate the team into groups with instructions to solve a complex puzzle using toys and sticks in order to build better communication. The only things that separate activities like these from kindergarten are cookies and a nap!

Sure, it's great to see everyone on your team laughing and having fun; it takes us back to the playgrounds of our youth. Why, even the company jerk is seen in a different light when the playing field (pun intended) is leveled for a day. But if and when you buy into these exercises, take them for what they really are: fun and games and a way to blow off steam. Because truth be told, the only way any of this could have a lasting effect would be if everyone working in the organization was a kid.

Companies, however, are made up of adults, each with a lifetime of experiences that have forged their personalities. And since most studies show that our personalities are pretty much set by the age of five, these team-building programs are nothing more than a classic exercise in futility. To actually think that an afternoon of catching people and building sculptures will change anyone long-term is a bit of a reach and, in my opinion, fairly ludicrous. After all, you don't run your company in the woods or from a playground, so when you return to the office, you'll get back to business as usual. People aren't falling off logs or trying to solve puzzles with toys and sticks; they are dealing with customers or working to resolve production issues. The daily grind of business and all of those agendas I spoke of earlier are waiting to wreak havoc on your day.

So now that I've completely trashed a large segment of the consulting market, here's how *I* believe you can get a team to perform and put the fun back into dysfunction. It's all about mission. If you establish a common focus that is achievable and in which everyone believes, you can become a high performance organization—period.

We see this kind of collaborative effort all the time in sports when championship games are played, or in medicine when teams of physicians come together to save a life. But in the world of business, the collaboration is somewhat more complex; there's no singular goal that every company shoots for, no Super Bowl or cure for a particular disease to rally people around. The goals differ from company to company and are as unique as the entrepreneurs who dream them.

Therefore, it's crucial that as leader of the pack, you're crystal clear as to where you want to go and by when. You also need to ensure that everyone in the organization understands your goals. You want a vision so lucid that everyone joining you will either gladly subordinate their personal agenda to yours because they believe that doing so will allow them to realize their dreams as well, or leave entirely. There can be no middle ground.

I am not advocating that companies be filled with people mindlessly following the leader at all times, because there's danger in that as well. You can have the most committed people in the world following you, but if they lack the talent and skills to get you there, you'll still fail. To see this in action, you need look no further than any large corporation that's enjoyed past success but is now openly struggling. I believe that these corporations tend to lumber around and fall short primarily because they adopt a Stepford wife mentality when it comes to hiring. Past success leads them to value sameness and sterility in their workforce, so they end up hiring a certain type of person—one who walks, talks, and thinks exactly like the current employees do—rather than selecting an applicant with the abilities and creativity needed for the future. This wonderfully homogenous workforce sees things through only one set of lenses and approaches all issues and obstacles in the same old way. That's why it misses the warning signs, doesn't see the curve ahead, and eventually ends up in the ditch.

While a well-thought-out vision should never be up for debate, the tactics and processes needed to get there should *always* be. This line of thinking brings into play another one of my favorite business isms about building high-performance teams: "If two people agree all of the time, one of them is useless." The last thing a true leader wants or needs is a company of yes-men and yes-women. That is why dysfunction in an organization should be measured not by the team members' ability to get along, but by their ability to produce results. After all, what good will it do your company to have the team members hanging out together at happy hour if they're not performing? The team's ability to perform and achieve its goals is the best way to determine if its behavior is a problem.

To put it simply, if the team regularly performs at a high level, it's probably a cohesive unit that understands and is comfortable with creative conflict. If not, the team is dysfunctional and needs to be improved. When attempting to fix the group's problems, remember that all high-performance organizations encourage individual creativity within an environment where everyone openly discusses and champions ideas. To be sure, disagreements and conflicts occur, but they are focused on the work to be done rather than on following someone's personal agenda. This makes it easier for all parties involved to compromise where necessary and make the right decisions.

Creative conflict within an organization also breeds a kind of awareness. When you focus your activities and conversations on the work to be done, a company's strengths and weaknesses become more obvious and easier to discuss. You're constantly holding a mirror up to the firm and saying, "This is exactly who we are, and it's OK." Because seeing the talent within the company for what it really is and accepting it makes setting up your team members for success easier.

This is why I always pay more attention to my company's—and employees'—weaknesses than I do to their strengths. This opinion was forged in every motorcycle safety class I've ever taken, because the instructors constantly stressed that we should be aware of our limits when on the road. Just because the person you're following can take the curve at 50 miles per hour doesn't mean you have to, especially if you aren't good enough!

## Talent Inventory

In order to properly function on the bike, I know that I must always maintain a realistic view of my abilities in relation to my performance edge—that danger zone beyond which I greatly increase the probability of a wipeout and jeopardize my well-being. Focusing more intently on limitations than on strengths reinforces that reality, because being dysfunctional on a bike is usually hazardous to one's health. And although we may not be taking curves at 50 miles per hour in business, we all have a distinct edge beyond which our chances of a wipeout increase dramatically. Unfortunately, most companies learn where their edge is too late to prevent problems, because they fail to get a good handle on what it is they are *not good at*. We've been taught to exercise our strengths, but any strength that's overused will become a weakness. There's often a very fine line between the two, and while strengths are usually self-evident, weaknesses often hide—or their importance is overlooked—until it's too late. This is why a clear understanding of your organization's weak points is crucial to successfully navigating your path.

As business leaders, we are accustomed to the process of physically counting inventory or periodically reviewing the effectiveness and usage of capital resources. But rarely do we stop to take inventory of the talent within our organization—a factor that has a direct effect on our team's ability to perform at the highest level. This review is needed because, as your company grows, the talent needed to sustain that growth must evolve in concert with the organization. For example, the skill it takes to manage a department of 3 is far different from the skill required for a department of 10 that in short order may become a department of 20. The larger the department, the farther away a manager gets from the actual work product, which requires different communication skills, different project-management skills, and so on.

As the types of management skills change, so does the type of worker. You often find yourself moving from employees who thrive in an environment of hands-on management to those who are self-starter types—and thus need less direct oversight. The wrong mix of talent can be a recipe for disaster—your company will not function well if you have a team of self-starters working for a true hands-on manager, or vice versa. Therefore, I submit that if your company has grown significantly and is over five years old, you must review the talent within it on at least an annual basis.

I therefore employ what I call a *Talent Inventory,* a process that helps to better identify the strengths and weaknesses of a team.

The importance of this process cannot be overstated. It is of little use to determine the tactics necessary to take you to your destination if your people are incapable of implementing them. The inventory isn't about identifying their personal shortcomings or weaknesses, as much as it is determining where their true talents lie. If somebody is struggling to consistently perform a particular task—but has a good attitude and is trying really hard—then he or she is probably facing a nontalent area. And that person's ability to ever become proficient at that task is slim.

The Talent Inventory is a simple process that begins with the department managers completing a simple Employee SWOT Analysis for each of their team members (see page 164). The managers are instructed to be as detailed as possible when listing the employees' Strengths, Weaknesses, Opportunities, and Threats. Listing Strengths and Weaknesses is fairly obvious. Under Opportunities we look for potential areas for advancement, improvement or new ways to help the company. Threats address areas where they can hurt the organization either through overt actions or their absence, i.e., no clear cut successor to someone in an area crucial to the company.

The managers then share the SWOTs in a meeting in which they openly discuss the analyses and provide each other with feedback. Holding this discussion in an open forum allows every manager to understand the amount of total talent within the organization and helps them when sharing employees on cross-company projects.

It is important that the discussion center on the employees' ability to function within the company as it moves forward, rather than focus on their past service and current performance. To be sure, performance to date plays a large part in the review process; however, consideration must be based primarily on their ability to grow along with and into the future needs of the company. I emphasize this because, too often, I see organizations

# Employee SWOT Analysis

Name: _____ Department:_____

Date: _____ Position:_____

## Strengths

_____
_____
_____
_____
_____
_____
_____
_____
_____
_____
_____

## Weaknesses

_____
_____
_____
_____
_____
_____
_____
_____
_____
_____
_____

## Opportunities

_____
_____
_____
_____
_____
_____
_____
_____
_____

## Threats

_____
_____
_____
_____
_____
_____
_____
_____
_____

**Comments:**

_____
_____
_____
_____
_____
_____
_____
_____
_____
_____
_____
_____

**Recommendations:**

_____
_____
_____
_____
_____
_____
_____
_____
_____
_____
_____
_____

Completed by:_____

held back by people in key roles who have outgrown their abilities. Therefore, I begin the discussion with this primary question:

*If the employee applied for the position today, would you hire him or her?*

If the answer is no, then we have a critical issue and must consider replacing this team member. If the answer is yes, then we move to the next question.

*Does the employee have the talent and ability to move to the next level within the organization?*

If the answer is no, the main concern becomes whether or not the employee will remain happy at the current level. It also gives the manager indicators to look for and address going forward. If the answer is yes, we then begin thinking of what the employee needs to improve on or develop in order to effectively move up. In either case, we move into the Professional Development Process with the employee (see Chapter 16).

Another benefit to discussing your findings, one on one, with each employee is that they begin to recognize and accept their own weaknesses and that of others. When everyone's strengths and weaknesses are out in the open, it's easier for a team member to raise his or her hand when help is needed and not have to worry about receiving a scarlet letter.

We strive to have the strengths of the organization balance the weaknesses whenever and wherever needed. High-performance companies understand that each employee is able to excel at certain tasks, but no one is good at *everything*. We all have a tendency to think, "I could be good at *that* if I just paid more attention to it or if I spent more time practicing it."

But the reality of the situation is that we're not good at something because it's simply not where our talent lies. If it did, we would be spending more time performing that task, because it would come more naturally to us. And your job as a manager is to identify what comes *naturally* to each worker in the company.

Again, it's all about the work to be done. I keep saying that, but it's so true. It's all about winning. You can't put people in positions where they don't have the ability to get the work done. Therefore, one of the key components of accomplishing the work to be done is for people and companies to identify what their weaknesses are.

This identification and discussion process doesn't happen overnight. It happens over time. That said, however, it shouldn't take more than 60 days to identify the more glaring weaknesses now that you are focusing on their most important areas of performance. You'll know after two months whether or not people are performing by the excuses being made and the delays in their projects, and that's when you might have to do a bit of reverse engineering to find out why.

Reverse engineering is determined by saying, "Here's the task you need to do." If it's done well, there's no issue. If it's not done properly or to the level of expectation, then you have to go back in and figure out why. What causes the performance to be inadequate? Is it a process-based issue inside the company? Or is it the fact that the worker just doesn't have the necessary abilities? If the answer leads you back to a personal characteristic of that individual, then you know you're probably dealing with a nontalent area.

When facing this situation with an employee, there are only three ways to work around it: (1) team the person up with somebody else, so the other's strengths can overcome those weaknesses; (2) build a process around the person to help overcome the weaknesses; or (3) move the person to a different place in the organization, or remove that person from the company altogether. Note that in order for this identification of dysfunction to work without destroying the morale of the organization, you must create an environment of trust where managers can and will buy into the concept. Managers in a high-performance organization flourish in an environment where there is a process that fosters understanding and support. Nobody gets chastised, and it becomes OK to openly discuss individual and team weaknesses because it's all for the good of the overall organization.

This is not about one person being better than another; it's simply about finding the best possible fit when performing a task or function. All workers are vital to the performance of the organization, and once they are OK with who they are and better understand their shortcomings, they can, as a team, devise a game plan to overcome them. If, as an organization, you know where your weaknesses are, you are better able to marshal your resources in order to achieve success.

## The Management Team

When dealing with dysfunction within any organization, I always begin working from the top down, because management sets the tone for the company. If the group members that are meant to lead aren't working well together, then it's safe to assume the rest of the organization is suffering from it. The Navigation Process is designed to expose and monitor the dysfunction within your management team so that you can better work within and around it. The Tactical Planning Process has provided you with the agreed-upon tactics needed to reach your goals, allowing you to better measure your team members' actions against the goals and discuss any issues in subsequent meetings.

To better understand and deal with team members' individual idiosyncrasies, I like to administer individual personality-profiles in which communication styles are identified. These are approved, certified tests, and they're uncannily accurate. The best example of how these tests can identify and resolve internal issues within a company happened early in my career, when I was called in by a CEO to handle an ongoing conflict between two senior managers in a local high-tech firm.

The problem was that Carl, the director of operations, and Jerry, the director of marketing, refused to work together, and their conflict was beginning to affect the entire company as lines were drawn and sides were taken. After my initial discussion with the CEO, my recommendation was not to single them out, but rather to work with the entire management team on their communication. From there, the main conflicts would surface and we as a team would work to resolve them. I began by interviewing all of the managers one-on-one and having them complete a simple personality profile; we then scheduled a meeting to discuss the results.

At the meeting, when we were covering the individual personality styles within the team, both Carl and Jerry looked at each other and began laughing. I stopped the meeting and asked what was so funny. Carl responded by pointing out that he and Jerry's styles were totally opposite, which, in turn, explained why there was so much conflict between them. It turned out that Jerry made choices quickly and tended to shoot from the hip, while Carl was much more thoughtful in his approach to decision making. Carl described how Jerry would come up with an idea and, moments later, blow into Carl's office and excitedly tell him all about it. Jerry would then spend the next minute standing in the doorway tapping his foot, waiting for a comment; he would then walk away frustrated at the perceived lack of interest on Carl's part. This had caused Carl to complain to the CEO that Jerry was always trying to "drive his damned ideas down my throat," while Jerry had complained that "Carl couldn't make a decision to save his life."

What they both immediately recognized in their respective profiles was not an unwillingness to cooperate on either of their parts, but rather a difference in communication styles. In order to avoid further conflict, they both agreed to a solution whereby it would still be OK for Jerry to approach Carl with his ideas in the future as long as he allowed Carl to take the appropriate time to think about them before responding. The team immediately responded to the change and productivity increased; the personality profile and discussion had squelched the conflict.

The real lesson here, for me, was that correcting dysfunction always hinges on communication. The better everyone understands each other's goals, the easier it is for the team to mesh. It's not that you're telling people something that they don't already know; instead, you're removing any blind spots they may have about their personality and style in handling issues. They begin to understand how their attitudes and actions affect not only those around them but the entire organization, and this knowledge leads to a more cohesive and productive team.

Once your organization identifies and deals openly with its dysfunction, people become less stressed about it. This is because you have lessened what I refer to as the *disappointment gap*—the delta between *your* (the manager's) expectations and the employee's limitations. The size of that gap directly correlates to the amount of disappointment you have in their performance. In other words, if we all know each other's strengths—and, better yet, if we all know each other's weaknesses—then expectations become more realistic.

You now set people up for success instead of failure; you no longer assign that introverted numbers person to customer service and agonize over the poor job performance. As a good leader, you understand that the market rarely allows you to stay in a comfort zone, which means that all team members need to stretch their abilities. But you need to enable them to do so without setting them up for failure in the process; having a clear understanding of their weaknesses allows you to better accomplish this.

Although you'll learn most of what you need to know about your people in the first 60 days after implementing your tactics designed in Chapter 12, the process of dysfunction identification is continual. I do this through one-on-one meetings, which are nothing more than structured conversations. Having individual, documented tactics allows for more focused conversations, which occur during the regularly scheduled one-on-one meetings I described in the previous chapter. Along with tracking my employees' progress, I also make it a point to ask them, "How's it going? What's getting in your way? What's working and what's not working?"

I've also learned to become more of an observer than a participant in group settings. I take good notes to supplement the information that my employees provide in their Update forms (as discussed in the previous chapter). This way, I can see new patterns of behavior as they develop and monitor old ones in order to ensure that my people work well as a team.

Once you put these principles into practice, will people still get upset at others in your company? Yes. Will people still let others down? Yes. But at least the people in your company will understand how and why. Because when you are aware of each other's imperfections and learn to work with them, you can really start having fun, because *now* the company will be accomplishing things. The main thing to remember when building a team is *fit*. Do your people fit the tasks and do they fit the team? The answer must be yes on both counts, because as I've said countless times in this book, it's all about the work to be done.

**Road Rules:**

- The best teams are built around a clearly defined mission, and harnessing the power of your team is a step-by-step process.
- Respect the role and respect the person.
- Conduct a talent inventory of your entire staff.
- Apply your staff's skills and abilities to the work to be done (the mission).
- Make sure your managers understand each other's personalities and communication styles.
- Observe your team; address any weaknesses and adjust your team as necessary to meet the changing needs of the organization.

*You can access my free tools to help you better Communicate, along with detailed instructions, on my web site at www.BikersGuidetoBusiness.com.*

 CHAPTER 16

# Sharpening Your Skills

*We now accept the fact that learning is a lifelong process of keeping abreast of change. And the most pressing task is to teach people how to learn.*

—Peter Drucker

When bikers ride on the open road, things come at them fast and they need to be prepared. Because of this, good bikers are always working on their skills by taking annual defensive driving courses, asking fellow bikers about road conditions, and constantly practicing their fundamentals. And once experienced riders achieve a certain level of proficiency, they seamlessly move from a training mode into more of a shared learning environment.

However, the word *teaching* implies that there's a one-way conversation between a teacher who knows all and a student who needs to learn it. A *learning environment,* on the other hand, is a situation where no teacher/student dynamic exists. Instead, two experienced people share their separate subject knowledge. An example of this in biking is when two riders both have experience riding in the rain, but one is more familiar with the particular road they'll be riding. A few key tips here and there from the more informed rider will be invaluable in increasing the other rider's awareness of the skills needed to make it to the destination successfully.

The same concept applies to experienced employees within any long-term business. Each is familiar with the overall company and its goals, but there are different viewpoints depending on department and position. In other words, sales can provide the rest of the company with invaluable information about market conditions, such as competing companies and products, that is crucial to steering the company in the right direction.

Simply put, in order to reach your destination successfully, you must build your organization's skills and abilities based upon where you are going, not where you are now. This is a mantra that I repeat to the people in my organization and to the clients with whom I work, and you will hear it repeated throughout this chapter. Too often, I see companies stagnate because their employees don't have the talent needed to make it to the next level. It is a fact of business that in order for a company to sustain solid growth, its employees and leaders must grow along with it.

## Professional Development

The best way I've found for a company to achieve and maintain top performance is to institute a Professional Development Process (PDP). The need for such a process isn't on most entrepreneurs' radar screen, because they're running small companies and are too busy working *in* the business to take the time to work *on* the business. There are simply too many everyday challenges that get in the way, and besides, that kind of analysis is for big companies.

For years, I didn't think an assessment like this was a good use of time because of the daily burdens that I faced as a company leader. But I've since come to understand that a Professional Development Process doesn't have to be complicated in order to be successful. I also knew while I was developing it that time is gold in an entrepreneurial company, so the process had to be both easy to implement and short on time commitment. In order to get results, it also needed to engage everyone and get all team members involved.

I needed a simple and consistent method of learning that matched the needs of the organization. I also wanted it to be versatile enough to implement in my client companies. That's why I built the Professional Development Process around three essential areas of development and understanding.

**Fundamentals.** This is information employees need to do their job well every day. Initial training is the foundation upon which successful, high-performing companies are built. This is the how-to part of an employee's learning curve, and nothing will run a high-growth company into the ditch faster than a lack of fundamental training.

**Advanced knowledge.** Employees need this information in order to develop *within* the company and expand beyond their current job functions. This is where you are looking ahead to the company's future and determining what skills the employees will need to match the company's needs as it grows. Failure in this area will have a negative impact on your forward momentum down the line.

**Awareness.** Your team members need information from *outside* the industry and their job functions, material that exposes them to the new methods, ideas, and techniques that are required for them to mature as businesspeople. I once read that in order to excel in today's business world, most of what we need to know lies outside of our industry or area of expertise. So you and your employees need to broaden your networks and scope of reading, because most business practices and methods can, with a bit of tweaking, be universally applied.

## How to Begin the PDP

As with everything in the Navigation Process, the PDP is driven by the work to be done, which will, at some point, require an upgrade in talent within the organization. Therefore, when I use the PDP in my own organization, my first step is to identify the skills and knowledge my workforce needs to develop in order to both get to that point and sustain success. (To do this when I work with clients, I have the managers outline the skills needed within the staff, and I have the CEO or owners outline the skills needed by the managers.)

Once these skills are identified, I then implement a thorough employee review process that includes the Employee SWOT Analysis described in the previous chapter.

Once the SWOTs have been completed and I have an idea as to where each employee fits, it's time to engage the employees. I do this by handing them a questionnaire that consists of three simple questions to determine where they want to go in the company:

- Where do you see yourself in three to five years?
- What are you doing to get there?
- What can I do to help you?

I tell the employees to take a week to think about and answer the questions. Once they have completed the questionnaires, I meet with them individually for a half hour to an hour to discuss their answers and growth opportunities for the coming year. In order to have more productive conversations, I also bring out their SWOTs and compare them to their perceptions. It's always interesting to see where it is the employee sees themselves and where it is they want to go. Often their perceptions differ from mine as to where they are (or are not) heading, and this gap represents the areas that need development.

The means of the employees' development can be as simple as cross-training or a seminar, or as involved as a program of college courses. What's most important here is to have an open and frank conversation about the future and their role in it. I also want to instill a sense of urgency in the process, because the quicker they begin developing their skills, the easier it will be for the company to grow.

Once the plan of action is agreed upon, I document it by capturing the specifics of the course of action we've agreed upon. I simply note the specific training the employee must complete, such as courses, seminars, and so on; the dates in the coming year by when these must be completed; and the desired results. It also has a place for the employee's signature and my signature, which turns it into a written agreement to a road map for improvement.

This document has many beneficial side effects. First, the employees always see it as a positive, which is good for morale. Second, it gives me a vehicle for constructive conversations with the employees in which we discuss their progress. Third, the employee and I have clarity as to the type and level of development needed in the coming year, which serves to close the disappointment gap. As I explained in the previous chapter, the disappointment gap lies between my expectations of my employees and their limitations. By openly discussing my expectations and their limitations, I can set them up for success rather than inadvertently setting them up for failure. This creates an atmosphere of honesty and safety, which results in a stronger bond between the employees and the company.

When you institute the PDP in your own organization, I recommend that you first implement it with the key managers reporting to you, in order to work through the nuances. Once you have the process down, have your managers identify the employees within their departments who need development, and then have your managers drive the process through your organization. The mutual accountability that this creates is killer.

## Mentoring

We've all had mentors in our lives, both inside and outside the companies where we've worked. And while I strongly believe in external mentors and advisors, I want to devote this section to the *tribal knowledge* within a company that serves as the framework for its business style and culture. Built over time, this organizational know-how represents the collective personal experiences of your employees—something that goes beyond written processes and job descriptions.

Collective information and experience is crucial to the success of any organization and greatly determines the speed at which you move toward your goals. So the last thing you want is for this flow of knowledge to be a hit-or-miss proposition. Unfortunately, in most entrepreneurial companies, this is often the case because the leaders do a poor job of transferring this crucial knowledge and experience throughout the organization.

A sure sign that you're not spreading the knowledge occurs when you wake up one day and find your company's most important information confined to just a few extremely valuable employees who, over time, have become indispensable to the company. The downside of this scenario is that as keepers of the knowledge, these employees can cause productivity to suffer or grind to a halt when they get overloaded or are absent.

It can be comforting, at first, to have individuals with so much experience, and everything works fine as long as you're on the same page. But everyone's agenda shifts over time, and these valued employees can quickly become a problem if they decide not to follow your direction. I wish I had a dollar for every time I heard a fellow entrepreneur complain about being held hostage by long-term employees whose demands have to be met simply because they cannot be easily replaced.

This is why it's *essential* that you implement a process that transfers all employee knowledge, regardless of length of service, throughout the company. And one of the most effective ways I've found to rapidly spread this knowledge, tribal or otherwise, throughout a company is with a formal *mentoring program.*

Yes, there are informal mentors in every organization, usually one or two approachable elders toward whom younger people gravitate for support and guidance. Having a few experienced employees available to take the younger staffers under their wings and impart their experience is essential to a company's growth. But mentoring shouldn't just roll down the mountain from the oldest and wisest; it needs to roll upward, too.

During his tenure as CEO of General Electric, Jack Welch understood the importance of learning from the younger staffers within the company and often asked them to mentor him in new areas. For example, when the use of technology began to grow within the corporation, he selected a twenty-something staffer as his mentor to help him better understand her generation's view of technology. This conversation afforded him great insight into the technology of the day and also showed him how his team could use it to improve productivity.

However, using Welch as an example isn't the best tactic when trying to get the point across to entrepreneurs. Few of us can relate to what goes on within a company the size of GE. But what is most important to remember is that mentoring isn't complicated, and it works in companies of all shapes and sizes. That's because at its core, mentoring is nothing more than two individuals coming together to share their experiences and insights through individual or group conversations. The only reasons you impose formality are to ensure that everyone has someone with whom they can talk, and to control how often these conversations take place. This approach gets every level of the organization involved and adds a much-needed consistency.

A formalized mentoring program has other benefits as well. The four partners of a CPA firm hired me as a consultant because they were facing a dilemma. They were great at recruiting talent out of college, but were finding it difficult to keep these employees for more than a year or so. Aside from the obvious cost of recruiting, hiring, and training, this turnover was negatively affecting the continuity within the team.

So we studied the comments made during exit interviews and discovered a trend. The majority of the first- and second-year associates were leaving the firm because of the 65- to 70-hour workweek required during the busy season. They thought it was crazy to work that hard, so they left in search of a saner workplace. We also conducted industry research and found, through talking with others within the accounting community, that many of the same individuals eventually left their *next* firm after a year or so—citing the same problem.

It wasn't until these people reached the third or maybe fourth stop along the way that they began to realize that this was the nature of the industry, and not just a characteristic of any one "crazy" firm. It would have been easy to simply chalk up their behavior to immaturity or to their unsuitability for the industry. But the reality of the situation went deeper than that; the phenomenon actually turned out to be a widespread societal issue.

During that time, a national TV news magazine did a segment on the new Millennial Generation and its problems integrating into the workplace. This younger generation has grown up in an ultracollaborative world where every child receives an award simply for participating. Win, lose, or draw, you get a trophy or plaque—so that no one goes home with low self-esteem. The problem with that touchy-feely world, however, is that those who've grown up in it never learned how to win. And they are now entering the toughest win-or-lose game there is: business. Only one person walks away with the contract, and as we all know, there is no second place.

This is why, when hitting their first busy season of 65- to 70-hour workweeks, these Millenials quit, and they thought that anyone who stayed was crazy for working so hard. Heck, I've even heard a story of one mother calling the manager and complaining that the company was working her son too hard! No wonder these younger employees didn't get a clue until their third or fourth firm. However, the entire situation gave the partners at my client CPA firm a clue.

Once we understood the problem, we quickly implemented a formal but simple mentoring program. The design upon which we settled required the employees at each level to mentor those at the level below, with the partners and more experienced managers mentoring multiple levels. A typical accounting firm, for example, has five levels of accountants:

- Interns or part-time college students majoring in accounting
- Associates or entry-level accountants in their first and second year
- Seniors or supervisory-level accountants
- Managers
- Partners

We began at the entry level, where we had the associates mentor the interns. The associates acted as the bridge into the company and gave the interns someone to go to for rudimentary, how-to work questions. This interaction also served as the "welcome to the family" stage, since the newest team members were quickly introduced into the social structure of the company through lunch meetings, happy hour, and other events.

The associates, in turn, were mentored by the seniors, an exchange that provided the associates with a better understanding of what they needed to do to advance their careers and handle more complex work. We then gave the senior- and manager-level employees a choice: Each could select someone from the level above them as a mentor. The more experienced associates also had the opportunity to choose, by ranking in order of preference, the individual they wished to mentor them. This was done confidentially through the human resources department; each eligible associate was required to list three choices, as no one mentor was allowed to work with more than three individuals.

Once the selections were approved, we held a formal training program for all mentors to discuss the dos and don'ts associated with mentoring. The goal was for every mentor and mentee to meet at least every 60 days to discuss everything from business to life. This way, everyone would learn not only how to become a better accountant, but also how to better embrace the lifestyle associated with public accounting.

In the years following the mentoring program's implementation, the firm has enjoyed tremendous double-digit growth. Three new partners have emerged from the pack, as well as a host of new managers and seniors. Retention, along with profitability and growth, has gone up significantly, making the firm an annual member of the local Top 100 Best Companies to Work For list. Now *that's* what I call harnessing the power of the pack!

## Books

Over the years, I've found that reading the right business book at the right time is an efficient and effective way to introduce new concepts and techniques into your organization. My love of books began at the age of five when, due to a temporary health problem, I had to get a shot in my backside every week for a few months. It wasn't so much that I was afraid of needles, but that I felt that being poked by a needle every single week was a bit much. So in order to get me to behave for the nurse and not yell, my mom promised to buy me a new book if I was good. And so, for the next few months (with the exception of one bad day with the nurse), I got that new book after each violation.

Although the shots eventually ceased, my love of reading never really went away. However, it was interrupted for an extended period of time—what I call my TV years, which ran from the age of 8 until around the time I turned 30. My affinity for literature was rekindled when a riding buddy and business associate rescued me from the idiot box by dropping off a copy of Peters and Waterman's *In Search of Excellence* (Harper Collins, 1st edition, 1982). That book immediately captured my attention and was the beginning of my odyssey with business books that continues to this day.

One book led to the next, and I've since devoured literally hundreds of business books. Name a situation in either business or personal development, and I've probably read about it—and can give you the title of two books that address it. Aside from making me more valuable as a Navigator, books open a world of new ideas, perspectives, and opinions that I'd otherwise not come across in my day-to-day life. Books are now as much a part of my daily life as the TV once was, and I always have two books going at a time. There's the one on my nightstand and another on a CD in the car. After all, why bother with talk radio or music when I can be listening to a brilliant businessperson?

Some of the books that I read are trendy, era-specific books du jour that have a finite shelf life, such as those from the dot-com boom days. But while their theories proved flawed in some ways, the lessons to be learned from comparing those past eras with the present are quite valuable.

And then there are the timeless classics, of which I have my favorites. These are required reading for all of my associates and client companies. The principles in these books are timeless and of immense value. Anything from the past written by Peter Drucker, or from the present written by Jim Collins, will always be part of my library. These books separate themselves from the pack and become wonderful references for learning and teaching.

The main thing to remember when introducing business books into an organization—whether it be my book or a classic written by Peter Drucker—is that they are nothing more than a compilation of the author's experiences and opinions. There are no silver bullets, and just because the theories in a book worked for GE's Jack Welch doesn't mean they will work for your company.

*How* you introduce books to your organization is also important. I learned early in my career that it wasn't enough to simply hand people a book and ask them to read it. It was a typical misstep that I often made: reading a great book myself and then buying a copy for others in the organization, thinking that we'd all be on the same page after reading it. A few weeks later, I'd ask what they thought of the book—only to find that it was never opened or they were interpreting it totally differently than I had. In either case, it was a misfire that hindered the progress I was seeking.

I then adopted a process that I use to this day: The books are handed out during a weekly meeting, and based on the length and complexity of the book, my team and I agree upon the number of pages or chapters we will read each week. We then incorporate time to discuss the book into our regularly scheduled meetings. It is during these discussions that we determine what, if anything, from its pages fits into the organization. I find that this method makes our meetings much more interesting, while keeping everyone on the same page both philosophically and tactically.

These weekly discussions turn into a focused case study on our company, in which we determine how to apply the concepts from the book to the organization. The typical business book is not more than 200 pages, so we can generally read it in its entirety in a month to six weeks. This means that in little more than a month, we are able to go from concepts on a page to reality within the company. And the discussion doesn't stop there—because the concepts we choose to implement become part of our Tactical Plan and are reviewed regularly in our standing meetings.

For example, a few years ago, I began working with the management team of a software company whose products are sold throughout North America. For most of its 25 years in business, the company had dominated its market, but it had almost cratered when the dot-com bubble burst in the late 1990s. The company found itself on the brink of bankruptcy and was forced to replace its CEO and begin a lengthy turnaround.

The initial phase of the turnaround was successful and the company quickly regained profitability. However, its problems were just beginning, because the next generation of its main product, counted on to fuel future growth, turned out to be severely flawed. The first customers to upgrade to the new software were experiencing horrendous problems and were screaming for the old version. But due to many factors, that request was impossible to grant, leaving the new CEO with no choice but to replace the leader of the development team.

When doing so, he brought in a strong chief operating officer to oversee operations overall as well as development. I came onto the scene shortly thereafter and watched as the new COO not only reconfigured his management team, but replaced over 60 percent of the operations staff as well. This massive change in personnel created an extreme culture shift; it became a company in which the old employees were pitted against the new. This meant that my job was to assist in melding the two sides—and turn them into a high-performance management team.

After settling on direction and focus, I worked with the COO to reconfigure the meeting and reporting structure, and then we turned our sights to quickly getting the new management team aligned philosophically. In order to get everyone on the same page—no pun intended—we implemented the weekly book review.

Now, while I like to introduce the same 8 to 10 books into my client companies, the order always varies according to

need. In this case, we elected to focus on communication because there was very little trust among the members of the new
management team, as well as throughout the entire operations
department. We began with a book that taught proven techniques on how to communicate openly and candidly. This was
a group of technology-minded managers (or geeks, as they're
commonly called), and this touchy-feely stuff was foreign to
most of them. So it didn't surprise me that the reading suggestion was met with extreme resistance. Everyone was overworked
and couldn't fathom having to read a book on top of everything
that they already had to do. The typical grumblings about "going
back to school" and "homework" were heard, but I knew from
experience that, over time, the employees would see the value
in the material we were covering and buy into the process.

I knew that, like many people nowadays, most of these team
members hadn't opened a book since school, so we began slowly.
We agreed as a group to cover two chapters (or approximately
40 pages) per week and to discuss what we'd read in our weekly
meeting. I also prepared a handful of PowerPoint slides with bullet points and key questions to help facilitate the discussion—and
to help those who had failed to read the material follow along.

This lack of buy-in happens in every organization, because
there are always team members who initially wait to see if the
new change sticks before getting involved. But it doesn't take
long before the nonreaders get with the program. Once they
hear fellow team members talk about the positive effects of
learning to implement the material, the knowledge becomes
contagious and they literally ask what the next book will be.

After the management team members had completed their
first book—which had them communicating at a higher level—
we decided to focus on process management. Here again, I
handed out a classic that dealt with identifying and handling
bottlenecks within the company, and I duplicated the process
that I had followed the first time around. I continued to create

PowerPoint slides, but this time we had 100 percent participation from the start and the team members aggressively dug into the material. The discussions became livelier as their improved communication skills took over, and we began to lay the foundation for long-term improvement.

At the time of this writing, we've covered six books and the company is enjoying solid profitability in an ever-changing marketplace. Since the turnaround began, serious competitors have entered the market, so in order to fend them off we've moved beyond the fundamentals and are now studying how to build a great company with great leaders who provide outstanding service to their customers.

I have another client who's gone far beyond the usual list of business books and now leads his management team through books on historic figures like Henry Ford and Benjamin Franklin. He understands the importance of expanding beyond business and sees that creating an environment of continuous group learning produces top-level performance. While today's business books are indeed extremely valuable, the classics take the team's knowledge and ability to think to another level. That, I dare say, is why it's no coincidence that this particular CEO is three times more profitable on a per-store basis than his nearest competitor.

As these case studies show, the time to introduce a particular book is determined by both the business's Tactical Plan and the issues faced during its implementation. The good news is that there are many, many excellent books out there that will meet your needs; you can see the list of my favorites on the *Biker's Guide to Business* web site at www.BikersGuidetoBusiness.com.

## Other Learning Opportunities

In order to achieve high performance, the three components of a learning environment I've described—the Professional

Development Process, a formal mentoring program, and books—should become part of the way you regularly do business. That said, there are many other options out there to supplement learning within your organization, such as seminars, speakers, conferences, and other resources. What follows are a few that I feel are worthy of consideration.

## Centers for Entrepreneurship

Most major universities now have centers for entrepreneurship, which are designed to foster entrepreneurship within the student body and the community. They are usually focused on established entrepreneurial companies, as opposed to start-ups. They offer a low-cost way to tap into some incredible programs, such as speakers, workshops, and college-level courses for employee development.

There are also opportunities for entrepreneurs to get free consulting provided by senior MBA students under the guidance of their instructor. The cool thing about this is that the students are usually older and members of the workforce, which brings a wealth of experience to your project. I've also known centers and universities that have partnered with corporations to design custom courses to fill specific needs; depending on the size of your company, this option could be worth looking into.

I personally work closely with a local college, Rollins College, to help design workshops and mentor female entrepreneurs through the Athena PowerLink program. But one of my favorite programs is one where we pull together a roundtable of six to eight CEOs to discuss a specific business topic. The room is then lined with MBA students who get to listen to the first half of the program, and then ask questions during the second half. This takes the information from the realm of theory and puts it into the realm of today's reality—very cool stuff.

If there's a center for entrepreneurship in your area, I highly recommend that you partner with it. It can be one of the most valuable relationships you form.

## Peer Groups

There are many organizations out there offering monthly peer group meetings, whether they are based on CEO, CFO, or COO level membership. I've both facilitated and participated in peer groups since 1994, and these meetings have been vital to my survival and eventual success in business.

In case you are unfamiliar with the concept, a group like this is comprised of peers—in my case, CEOs—who gather monthly to discuss the major issues that they and their organizations face. It's our one opportunity to openly share our deepest, darkest fears and problems with a group of people who've not only been there, but may be experiencing the same problems at that very moment. These are issues we dare not reveal to others in our organizations, because most of the time, they won't understand—or we'll end up scaring the daylights out of them.

The best peer groups are led by a paid facilitator, with a size that can range from as few as 6 members to as many as 16. My recommendation is to join a group with no more than 8 members, since there are only so many hours in a meeting, and if there are too many people in the room, you run the risk of not discussing your issue that month.

Also, make sure that the other members are all at your peer group level. In other words, if you are the CEO of a 15-year-old company, make sure you're not joining a group of start-ups. Having the other members in a situation similar to yours ensures a good discussion and constructive feedback at each meeting. It is also vital that there is total confidentiality; you need a safe environment in which to discuss the inner workings and trade secrets of your company.

There are also peer group opportunities for key team members, such as your CFO, COO, director of sales, and director of human resources. Having them join a peer group is a great way to enhance their development while bringing an outside perspective into your organization.

## Coaching

For the past six years, I have had a wonderful business coach, whose main job is to make me accountable, since as CEO of my organization, I am accountable to no one but myself. Sure, I have a duty to my clients and my company, but at the end of the day, if I want to turn left, I go left. However, I am totally answerable to my coach.

Twice a month, we have meetings during which she tracks my progress and helps me to make plans and set priorities. She is not afraid to challenge my thinking, and she calls me out on unfinished tasks or lack of productivity. I look to her for insight as well as information from outside of my box. It's not uncommon to receive a book or Web link within days of our meeting that specifically addresses something from our discussion.

The main benefit a coach brings into my world is a consistent conversation. She is the only one who literally tracks along with me and knows, at all times, 90 percent of what's happening in my life. And that is invaluable.

## Consultants

By now, you are fully aware of the fact that I am a business consultant. That said, however, my clients and business associates alike refer to me as the "anti-consultant" because of my methods and my attitude toward consulting in general. To be sure, there are many great consultants out there in the marketplace, and

I firmly believe that if you have a specific project that needs guidance, or if you aren't large enough to employ a world-class talent full-time, then you should rent it.

The key to a successful relationship with a consultant, however, is to understand the nature of the relationship, and this begins with knowing *why* you really need one and exactly what it is that you need him or her to do. You have to stick to that plan, because consultants are far too often hired to do *one thing*—and then they unpack their bags and stay awhile, completing tasks beyond their original scope of work. In other words, you must know what success will look like before you hire someone. You have to set definite, measurable goals, such as "My sales will increase by 10 percent in one year" or "I will have a fully mapped process for product development within 60 days." In my case, my clients know that the nature of our relationship will be long-term and will revolve around a five-year plan. Therefore, I usually find myself navigating their organization for at least that amount of time. To be sure, there are breaks in between—because no one should be in your organization for that long—but we tend to reconnect at some point.

Whether the gig is short-term or long-term, once you contract with a consultant, your job is to keep him or her focused. If you don't, you may wake up one morning to find the consultant has gone beyond the original scope of the work and is now creeping into other segments of your organization. Before you know it, you're paying double what you originally intended, without receiving double the benefits.

Yes, there may be reasons that justify the consultant's moving into an area that was not originally contracted for. But discuss this new development thoroughly, and compare it to your Tactical Plan. If it's necessary for the execution of the plan, then do it; if it's not, don't. Never begin to fix a segment of your organization just because it sounds like a good idea. Stay true to your plan, because *hiring a consultant at the wrong time is worse than not hiring one at all.*

> *How you choose to implement the tools and tactics listed above will be unique to your organization so don't worry about style. Just focus on establishing a consistent method of learning because you'll not achieve sustained high performance without it.*

 **Road Rules**

- Only a strong learning organization can take full advantage of the changing marketplace.
- Design a formal but easy-to-implement learning plan for your organization and people.
- Knowledge should flow naturally throughout your organization.
- Base the plan on what's needed to implement the tactics necessary to reach your goals.
- Create a Book of the Month Club.

---

*You can access my free tools to help you Sharpen Your Skills, along with detailed instructions, on my web site at www.BikersGuidetoBusiness.com.*

CHAPTER 17

# Your Role as Road Captain

I've written this book with the intent of helping you success-fully get where you truly want to go. The days and weeks roll by quickly, so you have to wake up and go for it each day, whether you're ready or not. In the previous chapter, I shared stories about how my clients and I use the tools, tips, and techniques in today's business books. It's important to note that just because I was successful in applying a certain technique in a particular way doesn't mean that's the only way to apply it, nor does it mean that you should strictly imitate the way in which I did so. And keep in mind that the worst thing you can do with the information in this or any other book is to take your team on a ride of experimentation.

When riding, I refuse to follow any road captain who changes direction at the drop of a hat, turning this way or that with little or no rhyme or reason. Unfortunately, I've of-ten walked into the offices of my client companies and heard horror stories of teams that felt like they were being forced to follow a poor road captain when their bosses pulled them in one direction or another depending on the latest book they'd read. Information and advice is a double-edged sword, and the way you choose to integrate them into your daily business life will determine whether you lead a smooth ride or one that few will want to follow. Therefore, I thought it best to close the book with a few dos and don'ts that can help you become a better road captain when leading your team. And as there are no absolutes, your style will dictate how you choose to use what I've written.

## Crash and Burn

When I first began working as a facilitator for CEO peer groups, I failed to see the danger in offering up absolute advice on someone else's issue. The other CEOs and I would listen attentively to our group member's issue and would then blurt out—right or wrong—our solutions with gusto, often with someone's future in the balance. At least once a meeting, we recommended that someone be fired or removed from a position while working with, at most, half the information necessary to properly make that decision. I still cringe to this day when recalling some of the feedback we gave.

This danger finally became apparent to me when a relatively new client named Glenn was unexpectedly forced by his partners from his position as managing partner in a local service firm. I'd been called in three months earlier to try and repair a breakdown in communication between him and his three partners. It wasn't until after his termination that I came to understand that the root cause of his dismissal lay in his membership in a CEO peer group facilitated by another consultant in town, who I knew, but with whom I was not associated.

The facilitator and members of this group were qualified, successful businessmen and businesswomen, so the problem had nothing to do with their credentials. It instead had everything to do with the insufficient information upon which they based their feedback. Glenn is an extremely persuasive leader, who does a great job of selling his ideas and rarely backs down from them. Therefore, the other CEOs on his team heard only his very passionate side of the story—and never had the benefit of hearing the flip side. Their feedback served to bolster Glenn's already intractable position, and armed with this validation from his fellow team members, Glenn fought tooth and nail to drive his ideas through the company. He couldn't comprehend why his partners disagreed, and they grew tired of his inability to listen. Resentment brewed and could no longer be ignored or overcome, so on a nondescript Tuesday morning Glenn's partners asked him to leave the firm and summarily bought him out.

Looking back on the entire situation, I am certain that, with the benefit of both sides of the story, Glenn's fellow CEO team members would have advised him differently. Instead, they unwittingly led him to his demise, which confirmed the age-old saying that "The road to hell is paved with good intentions."

The lesson here is that there are always two sides to a story and reality always lies somewhere in the middle. When we discuss an issue with someone, the advice we receive is only as good as the information we've given. We are also incapable of truly laying out both sides of the story, so whenever you receive feedback from a trusted advisor (or glean something from a business book), it's essential to stop and take the time to filter it. Does it feel right to you? What will the members of your management team think about this change, and how will it affect them?

As entrepreneurs, we are often called upon to make decisions in a vacuum or to go from the gut. But when you seek to introduce changes into your organization that may radically affect how it's run, you *must* listen to feedback. If your partner or management team still disagrees, ask yourself why. Because unless you're surrounded by stupid people, there is probably a valid reason for the disagreement. Make sure you stop long enough to fully understand and appreciate the opposing position. After all, why bother to have these people around you if you're not going to listen to them?

## The Importance of Style

I have certain friends who I don't ride with often, mostly because of their style. One of my closest friends, for example, turns into Evel Knievel when he's in the saddle. We'll take off for a nice, leisurely Saturday morning ride, and the next thing I know, he's leading us to the interstate so he can blast off at 90 miles per hour. No matter how hard I try to get him to, he won't slow down and absolutely cannot follow any speed that isn't at or near his liking.

As a result, we rarely ride together, and not simply because the speed at which he rides is dangerous. His love of biking has more to do with speed than with enjoying the surroundings and experience of the journey. Unfortunately, he's not alone, as many of my other friends are addicted to the rush associated with going fast on two wheels. Now, I'm not totally against going fast in the right instance, but for me, riding is all about slowing down and being in the moment. I want to see things for the first time along a path I've ridden a hundred times.

In the end, neither of us is wrong; we just approach riding differently. So when I elect to saddle up next to these friends, I know what I'm in for and I accept it. There are segments of the ride where I'll hang with them, but over the course of a day-long, 150-mile ride, our individual styles eventually win out—and we become individuals on bikes rather than a team. They eventually blast ahead, while I hang back and ride *my* ride.

The danger here occurs if I, the slowest of the riders, have a problem with my bike and need their assistance. By the time it dawns on them that I'm missing, a hundred things could have gone wrong and a lot of time could have gone by. With cell phones and roadside assistance, biking problems today are more easily overcome than in the past. However, try translating the issue of varying riding styles to the health of your business. Do the different approaches within your organization mesh and complement yours? Certainly, you don't want only slow-lane riders in your organization or only speedsters; a proper mix is necessary. Just note that things will run more smoothly if your team members' styles complement yours—especially when you introduce changes or tackle problems.

My years of riding have taught me that there's more than one way to ride up a mountain. In my business travels, I've often watched two entrepreneurs in the same industry approach similar issues in vastly different ways—and seen them both succeed. In each case, their success came from understanding and staying true to their individual styles, which allowed them to simply be who they are, day in and day out.

If a suggested solution calls for you (or the member of your team handling the problem) to do something out of character, think twice about it. If you aren't a real "people person" and the solution requires that you leave your office for extended periods of time to shake hands and slap backs, you'll eventually fail. This is like my 90-mile-per-hour ride—I'll do it for a while, but over time, I'll revert back to my true nature and do what I'm most comfortable with. Similarly, the more you introduce changes that go against your style, the less chance you have for real change to stick. All of the initial effort will be lost, because your team will just wait for you to quit and go back to the status quo.

All great road captains know that the more complex the problem facing the group is, the simpler the solution needs to be. They are consistent in their approach, which allows those who follow them to have a more enjoyable ride and get to their destination safely and on time.

## Connecting with Your Team

The best example of connecting with a team comes from a father and son who also affected the best transition of leadership I've seen in business. This story isn't about that transition, but rather their innate ability to communicate with their team in such a way that, over a span of 40 years, they built a company of over 400 people that felt like a company of 50.

Shortly after signing on to consult for their organization, I traveled to each of its five branches across the state. My assignment was to identify the needs of these distant locations so that the home office could better serve them. When the topic of communication came up, I heard the same story over and over again. In the early days, Joe (the father) was the main salesperson and covered the state, driving business into the branches. This was in the days before he could publish his travel schedule in Outlook, so he'd usually pop into the branch unannounced to touch base with the troops when he was in their area.

The team members at the branches told the story of a tired CEO pulling into the parking lot at 4:45 with his tie half undone after a long day of sales calls, carrying an ice chest of beer. Everyone from the branch manager to the mechanic's assistant would gather round, grab a cold one, and have a laid-back conversation with Joe. In fact, it wasn't that long ago that the CEO himself was tugging a wrench alongside most of them on jobs, which allowed the employees to share the trials of the day and stories of the jobs they were currently working on. They covered serious issues at times, but mostly they laughed and joked about the inside happenings of the company. They talked about what was going on with their individual lives and families, and all the while, a culture was being built, stop by stop, and beer by beer.

Fast forward to the late 1990s—and eldest son Don is in year three of his five-year transition into the role of CEO. Having begun his career in the company at the age of seven, sweeping out the shop on weekends and after school, Don had held almost every position within the company and was extremely well respected. Everyone knew he shared his dad's passion for the business and its employees. However, there was one small hitch. Don wasn't quite as easygoing and outwardly friendly as his dad, and it wasn't his style to show up with a six-pack and chat. But he knew something was lacking in the area of communication, and my interviews confirmed that he needed to find his own way to touch his employees.

The question was how. Don was very clear about the fact that he wasn't going to pretend to be his dad and show up with that six-pack. Heck, even if he wanted to, it wouldn't have had the same impact as when Joe had done it. Don's dad was more than the former CEO; he was company founder and a larger-than-life figure in the industry. So instead, Don decided to keep it a bit more formal and implemented Pizza with the Pres. This entailed visiting each office once a quarter with a load of pizza and eating lunch with everyone while he fielded questions and chatted with his employees.

Lunchtime fit Don's style better than happy hour and allowed him to be more comfortable, which helped his employees to see him as a genuine leader who cared. To this day, the lunches connect Don to the company in a way that daily computer reports cannot. It should therefore come as no surprise that during Don's tenure as CEO, the organization has doubled in revenue and continues to be one of the best in the business.

On the flip side of this story is the tale of Greg, who around the same time as Don, assumed control of his father's 40-year-old company. There was only one location, and at the time of the transition Greg's dad spent about 50 percent of his time out in the community serving on one board or another. Over the years, he'd become a pillar of the community and was able to fill this role primarily because he had spent years establishing a strong infrastructure while Greg was behind him running the day-to-day.

Like Don, Greg had worked his way up through the ranks of his dad's business and knew it well. But unlike Don, when taking over from his father, Greg failed to identify those all-important connection points that were needed to successfully drive the company forward. He quickly filled his old position of sales manager with someone from outside the organization and assumed his father's position in all functions. He sat on all of the boards, networked within the community, and eventually became president of the local chamber of commerce. While these were all worthwhile roles, few had a direct impact on the business.

Unfortunately, these positions left Greg with little time to properly train and oversee his replacement, a situation that led to a revolving door with one hire after another diving into the fray and eventually failing. As a result, turnover in the department began to skyrocket as more and more salespeople quit due to lack of direction. It didn't take long for the business to begin losing market share, and sales dropped steadily over the next few years.

Greg looked everywhere for help in stemming the tide and eventually joined a CEO peer group, which advised him to step down from a board or two in order to spend more time rebuilding his sales infrastructure. But since the feedback wasn't what Greg wanted to hear, he didn't apply it and soon left the group. He continued to look everywhere but in the mirror, and by the time he realized that what the company needed most of all was his direct involvement, it was too late.

The lesson here is that instead of taking the time necessary to forge his own identity within the company, Greg simply assumed his dad's identity, temporarily enjoying all of the trappings that came with the position of CEO. But by not earning his stripes and paying the dues necessary to properly take over the top position, Greg only succeeded in killing a profitable longstanding company. Remember, the dues you pay in getting to the next level aren't the same ones needed to stay there.

## Personal Touch

I am often contacted by entrepreneurs who are desperately trying to figure out how to stop their messages and goals from being dramatically watered down—or totally misinterpreted—by those responsible for delivering them throughout their organizations. To be sure, part of the issue is the overdependence on today's numerous avenues of communication. Nothing can screw up the meaning of a message faster than the overuse of e-mail, text messaging, voice mail, and the occasional fax.

When on the road, the road captain has many ways of communicating with his riders. However, it's the person-to-person discussions at fuel stops that let him know their condition at all times. If the weather or terrain changes when riding the road ahead, it's vitally important that he understand their experience levels and the speeds at which they are most comfortable.

In business it's vital, especially for entrepreneurs, that you know firsthand the same types of things about your team. As we've seen, the best leaders maintain close personal contact with all levels in their organization. Unfortunately, they frequently confuse delegation with communication. It isn't enough for you to tell your director of operations what needs to be done—you also have to loop around and check to see if the people at the levels below have heard and *understood* your entire message. It's also important to find out if, along with understanding your message, they have everything they need to act on it.

My client Fred learned this lesson the hard way. When he restructured his organization, he cut his direct reports down from five to two: his CFO and his director of operations, Sam. He thought that by reducing the team to his two most trusted leaders, his messages to the rest of the organization would be crisper, which would lead to better communication throughout the company.

The move appeared to work for the next year or so, but things eventually began to unravel. Fred and Sam began to differ philosophically, which resulted in Sam significantly altering the content of Fred's messages to the midlevel managers. When Sam disagreed with directives from Fred, he did not present them to the managers as coming from the executive team (of which Sam was a key member); instead he presented them as coming from someone named "him" (Fred). This change in wording opened a crack that became a chasm and threatened the very future of the organization.

Over time, Sam simply moved the managers in the direction he wanted to go by stonewalling Fred's requests for information or by burying Fred's orders behind other, more pressing priorities. It must be said right here that both men were totally committed to the success of the organization; the problem was that each had a different idea of how to get there. The trouble was that by blindly trusting Sam, Fred had lost touch with his old middle managers and hadn't gotten to know his new ones. This led Fred to become more and more frustrated with the organization's lackluster performance, and during his weekly executive team meetings he began to openly question the team's talent, along with its ability to take the company forward.

When I stepped in, I recommended that Fred begin reconnecting with his middle managers by attending the weekly meeting that Sam chaired. This caused yet another dilemma: When Fred saw the level of talent in the room, he realized that the problem wasn't necessarily with the middle managers, but rather with Sam. Once he recognized this fact, the problem seemed to be a simple one to solve—remove Sam from the picture and begin working directly with the managers to get the company back on track. But that would be easier thought than done, mainly because the managers didn't really know Fred. They'd been insulated from him for years by Sam.

To address this issue, we implemented an internal hands-on campaign of sorts in which Fred began to attend more of the managers' meetings and engaged the team in both philosophical and tactical conversations. He then scheduled a series of one-on-one meetings with each manager over lunch or coffee, and began getting to know each of them individually. However, this internal campaign only brought about confusion among the managers, not so much over the company's direction or focus, but over whom they were to listen to.

It was painfully obvious that Sam and Fred were no longer on the same page philosophically. The rift quickly became personal, making it inevitable that one had to go. Sam was eventually asked to leave the organization, and while his talents are sorely missed, the divisive nature of his management style is not. This entire situation could have been prevented if Fred had not trusted so faithfully in the traditional organizational hierarchy. Unfortunately, he thought that he would be overstepping boundaries by talking directly to Sam's reports instead of going through Sam.

Fred and Sam's situation highlights the importance of understanding that the days of leading a company by going through strict channels—where employees are expected to "do what they are told"—are long gone. Today's generation of workers are accustomed to collaboration. These employees recognize their leaders not by a block on an old organizational chart, but rather by daily personal contact. So never, ever lose touch with your team.

## Forks in the Road

The story of Fred and Sam's conflict is a great example of how every ride has a beginning and an end. On bikes, it starts with the group meeting at a local breakfast spot or service station, and ends with the riders peeling off, one by one, at their exits to head home. The ride captain always knows this, so it's never a surprise when one member of the group pulls off and heads in a different direction.

Earlier in the book, I compared life and business to one long road trip and explained that the secret to a successful ride in each is identifying the exits you want to take. This philosophy also holds true for those who work for and with us. Unfortunately, we are often so intensely focused on our own exits that we rarely recognize when key team members reach theirs, which usually makes these events a surprise. This inevitable fork in the road comes in many forms and may occur for many reasons, including differences in philosophy, deficiencies in talent, inability to change, or lack of passion. We all know these departures are coming; the hard part is not taking them personally.

As in Fred and Sam's case, the warning signs of an impending fork in the road are usually there for months (and are always visible if you pay attention); however, they are easily overlooked. The easiest way to determine if you're facing a true fork in the road is to perform a litmus test, as in science class. Look for the work being done, and answer the following questions:

- Is it being done on time and to the level you want?
- If not, why? Is it because of a difference in philosophy?
- Do your employees have the talent required?
- Are they resistant to change, or do they no longer care?

If you answer yes to any of these questions, have a conversation with your team members immediately, if not sooner! Try not to get wrapped up in their personal issues or feelings. Remember, this is simply about the work to be done. You are in the business of providing your product or service; you are *not* in the savior business. Leave that to a pastor or professional counselor. Way too much time and money are wasted on managers' attempts to salvage people who, two years ago, were model employees. How they function *now* is who they truly are; if they aren't performing at the level you need—if the answers to the questions above don't give you that warm, fuzzy feeling that they can and will get there—then you need to sever the relationship *now*. Decisions to retain your employees should be based not only on past loyalty and performance, but on their ability to perform in the future.

Forks in the road are a natural part of your business's evolution and should be accepted as such. You can't take these events personally, because there's literally nothing you can do when faced with one. The only approach that you can take is to part amicably and go on your respective merry ways. The sooner you recognize these partings as inevitable and accept them, the sooner you can move along and reach the level of performance you're looking for.

 **Road Rules**

- It's your ride—get back to having fun.
- Stay true to your style.
- Remember, you are the only constant in the company. Everyone else is temporary.

# CONCLUSION

*When you discover your mission, you will feel its demand. It will fill you with enthusiasm and a burning desire to get to work on it.*

—W. Clement Stone

When you see a group of bikers rolling down the road, it's safe to assume that they all pretty much represent different walks of life. Heck, meet me at any bike fest and we'll hang out with accountants, lawyers, doctors, mechanics, carpenters, and real-rough riders. We come together to celebrate the culture of riding; we come to exercise our passion. It's the same thing in business, and when you see a group of passionate businesspeople—all with a great desire to get where they want to go—it's a beautiful thing.

I opened this book talking about passion and I'll end with it as well, because everything that I've told you is nothing without it. Passion is what sets us apart as entrepreneurs and what fuels our desires. The quote at the top of this page by renowned businessman and author W. Clement Stone speaks to the importance of focused passion. It is my hope that the insights and principles I've shared in *The Biker's Guide to Business* have given you a more focused approach to the day-to-day road course that is your life as an entrepreneur.

Remember, passion can thrive only in an environment where things are accomplished. Whether it's your business life or your personal life, passion and mission cannot prosper without each other. So it always comes down to the work to be done, and to you, as the leader, saying clearly and with absolute determination:

*This is my company.*

*This is our culture.*

*And this is where we are going.*

**Because happiness comes when we turn our passion into performance!**

Keep the rubber side down and enjoy your ride!

 MORE RULES OF THE ROAD

Throughout this book, I use a number of what my clients call my "bikerisms." In much the same way that top-level athletes use key phrases to reset their focus, my clients have used these maxims to maintain focus and stay on the right path. In that light, I thought it might be of value to list some of my favorites along with some thoughts on them.

## Happiness Comes When We Turn Our Passion into Performance

We are usually most passionate about what we are good at, which fuels our desire to do more of it. In both your business and your personal life, identify what you are most passionate about, focus on it, and become excellent at it. It'll put a smile on your face.

## Understand the In-Between

We can all identify where we are today, and most of us can identify where we want to be in the future. Successfully getting there, however, is entirely dependent on your ability to map out and focus on the in-between. All of your plans and subsequent actions must take place within the context of where you want to go. If these actions aren't going to move you closer to your goal or at least set you up to get there, you need to ask yourself why you are taking them.

## The Key to Success Isn't Recognizing Opportunity, but Instead Recognizing the Opportunities You Should Not Chase

Entrepreneurs possess many assets, none of which are greater than their ability to see opportunity. But is a particular opportunity right for you? Does it fit into your in-between and match your mission? And even if it is right for you, do you really need to chase it *now?* Nothing will derail a company faster than chasing the wrong opportunity or following the semi-right opportunity at the wrong time. In other words, be sure before you head down that path.

## Life and Business Are Two Sides of the Same Coin

I've read books by many so-called experts and life coaches who recommend that we "leave our work behind" at 5:00 p.m. on the dot. That's one of the most ridiculous statements I've ever heard. We're entrepreneurs, for goodness sake! Our business is our *life's passion* and the place where we spend most of our waking hours. When we're not *at* the business, we're thinking about it. The key to making it work is to accept this fact and control it, while making apologies to no one. Find your balance and be happy.

## It's as Much about Balance as It Is about the Finish Line

This maxim dovetails with the previous one. In order to find that elusive balance, you must first understand that it's different for everyone. Like an image that may seem pornographic to one person and be perfectly acceptable to another, balance is subjective and has no single standard. Only when you determine where *you* need to go and how quickly you need to get there can you better determine the amount of energy and time you need to expend. There isn't a single person or engine that is designed to run at full capacity and speed all the time, so make sure that you allow yourself to cruise a bit once you reach that finish line.

## Potential versus Success

These are, in my opinion, the two most misunderstood words in business. Sure, your company may have the potential to become a huge organization. But at what cost? And what does the *other* side of your life need?

Look at your life as a whole before blindly chasing business potential. Why spend time—that could be better devoted to your personal happiness—building a monster organization when a smaller and more manageable one will do?

## Speed of the Leader = Speed of the Pack

Your team members are watching you. If you're passionate, they'll be passionate; if you accept mediocrity, so will they. You set the pace—so never be afraid to set the bar too high. After all, they just might reach it.

## It's Not about Overcoming Fear, but about Understanding and Embracing It

Issues and conflicts come up all the time in business and they cannot be avoided. I've always found that problems turn out to be smaller the closer you get to them, so I suggest you adopt the habit of running toward problems and not away from them.

## Business Moves at the Speed of Life

Our best-laid plans are always affected by the fact that life itself takes precedence over all. Whether it's your own personal situation or one that's facing a team member, stuff is going to happen that will bottleneck your company from time to time. Understand it, accept it, and work around it; there is no other choice.

## It's All about the Work to be Done

Although personal agendas are a fact of business life, the ultimate goal is to perform the work. You need to make sure your team members keep this in mind so that they make the right *business decisions* when the outside world gets in the way. They should always be aware of their roles and the level of performance that's needed for the team—and the overall company—to achieve the goal. Ensuring that your team members understand these requirements is the best way I've found to reinforce responsibility and accountability throughout the company.

## Fit Matters

Talent is vitally important on any team. However, I'd rather have someone with 80 percent talent and 100 percent team skills than someone with 100 percent talent and only 80 percent team skills. You only have to look at certain professional sports teams that, year after year, purchase the best talent money can buy, only to lose again and again. In order for your team's focus to remain on the work to be done, the spotlight always has to be on the team rather than on an individual member.

## Business Is Easy—Until You Add People

People are always the wild card in any business. When you are the only person performing a task, you have total control over its outcome. But add one more person into the mix and you no longer have control; in fact, the best you can hope for is influence. Therefore, your ability to lead and manage people will determine your team's level of performance and success.

## You Never Know What You've Got until You Watch It

It's easy for people to alter the way they do things in the short run. But unless this change totally fits their personalities, they will revert to who they really are over time. Too often, I see leaders fall head over heels in love with a budding superstar's performance—only to wonder what went wrong six months later when their new star has become mediocre. Unless there are extenuating circumstances, *the current level of performance* is the indicator of a person's true abilities.

## If Two People Agree All of the Time, One of Them Is Useless

High-performing organizations create and then thrive in an environment of candor. Even if you're an egomaniac, you're doing yourself and the company a great disservice by surrounding yourself with yes-men. You can't possibly see all things at all times, and if you don't make it okay for them to disagree and dialogue with you, there's a ditch with your name on it.

## True Character Comes Out in a Crisis

Watch to see how your team members perform under fire. Do they take shortcuts or make the tough choices? Are their decisions, regardless of the pressure, made for the good of the company? Pressure is never an excuse, but it's a great measuring tool.

## Communication Ain't Always Pretty, but It's Always Communication

I've had the pleasure of working for and with many great leaders, each with their own style of communicating. Their styles ranged from subtle to totally in-your-face, and where I didn't always like their methods, they were still communicating to me. Therefore, in order for me to be successful, I had to look past their styles in order to *get the message*.

## Knowledge Isn't Power until You Apply It

In my life I've run across too many brilliant losers to count. They have all the answers and know it all, but they're too afraid to make a mistake and just can't pull the trigger when it counts. I always forgive errors of commission, because at least in these cases someone tried to *do* something. On the flip side, I always get rid of someone for errors of omission; they knew what needed to be done, but simply didn't do it. That is always inexcusable in my mind.

## Size Does Not Equal Significance

Peter Drucker said many great things in his lifetime, and this, to me, is one of the most profound. None of the major computer manufacturers took a college kid named Michael Dell seriously when he began selling computers out of his dorm room. By the time they recognized the threat, he had gained momentum and became an unstoppable force in the industry. Is there someone in your industry doing something really cool that you should pay attention to?

# THE MAN BEHIND *THE BIKER'S GUIDE TO BUSINESS*

Dwain M. DeVille is the founder and CEO of WaterMark International, Inc., a consultancy that serves business leaders. Watermark's approach centers around the art of Navigation, an innovative process Dwain developed to guide businesses small and large through the challenges they face when trying to reach the next level of performance.

Dwain began his career in the financial services and banking industry. The 15 years he spent in this field gave him a solid background in management, product development, commercial and retail lending, community development, and government relations.

Over the past 13 years, Dwain has worked with more than 100 start-up and growing businesses. He has developed a keen awareness of the pitfalls that these enterprises often encounter. He is known for his laid-back, engaging style, which enables him to connect with people in all levels of an organization. This style adds value to the equation and has helped him earn the respect and trust of his clients.

Dwain's Navigation Process plays a critical role in helping an organization reach its potential. This process not only defines an end goal, but also provides the tools and tactics to bridge the gap between *here* and *there*. The Navigation Process also defines the *how* and the *why*, providing the definitive road map that many organizations sorely lack.

Using a practical, hands-on approach, Dwain helps an organization deal with issues in a way that corresponds to its own style, culture, and timetable. As he works within that framework, he helps key players recognize problem areas and coaches them to become better decision makers and communicators.

While much of his work focuses on helping entrepreneurs and small business owners, Dwain's work for larger corporations includes team building, succession planning, mergers and acquisitions, and communication issues.

Dwain is an active community leader and volunteer in central Florida, where he serves on several task forces and boards.

As much as Dwain loves the challenges of business, he loves to ride his motorcycle even more. Last year, while enjoying a high-country Colorado tour, Dwain decided the time had come to combine his two passions, so *The Biker's Guide to Business* was born.

Dwain rides regularly, both solo and with groups, and has toured many parts of the country. After all the miles he's traveled, the appeal of motorcycling remains as strong to him today as it was when he first threw his leg over that Honda 100.

 INDEX